Winning the Fame Game

*How to Deal with Celebrity and Stay
Grounded, Admired, and Inspired*

by Valery Satterwhite

Redcat Editions
Redondo Beach, CA
© 2014

Published in the U.S.A. 2014 by
Red Cat Editions, Redondo Beach, CA

© Valery Satterwhite 2014

www.FameMentor.com

ISBN-13:   978-0-9821878-6-9
ISBN 10:   0-9821878-6-6

Designed by Aaron Drucker for Pen & Paper Digital.
Printed by CreateSpace, Charleston, SC.

To my extraordinary clients and all those who dare to ride the dragon of fame.

Your individual gifts, talents, and fortitude are the greatest expressions of the human spirit. We are forever enriched by your grounded, admired, and inspired presence.

Table of Contents

Fame is empowering. My mistake was that I thought I would instinctively know how to handle it. But there's no manual, no training course.

– Charlie Sheen

Foreword

Some years ago I remember meeting an aspiring actress at a party next door. It came out in conversation that I'd written and produced a few films that helped launch the careers of a few actresses. She asked if I was still a friend with any of them. I used to be friendly with Sandra Bullock. Not anymore? No. Why not? I don't know. I said something like: "When you become a star, something happens."

Well, the actress was appalled. It was as if I'd been used and discarded. But I didn't feel that way. And trust me, I'm not above being bitter and vindictive in the right circumstances. I just didn't have those feelings for Sandie. Mostly, you just grow apart, but to some degree, you're pulled apart. Fame has a way of doing that. No matter how grounded you are, you cannot resist at least a little change. I get it, in some way, what minor, 3rd degree celebrity status I've achieved has changed me to some degree.

Well, the actress refused to accept that, insisting that if she were to become a star (after being in one of my movies, of course) she wouldn't act like that, she'd still be my loyal friend. Maybe so, but I explained to her that Sandie didn't owe me anything. And it's not like she's denying me a kidney or anything. And it wasn't my movie that turned her into a star. It was more of a stepping-stone, but I didn't feel particularly stepped on. And then I pointed out to her that if and when she does become a star, she too will change. And it's not the fame that changes you, but the way people treat you.

When you're a celebrity, you suddenly get the unconditional love, respect, and admiration of millions of strangers. And if you grew up in a household where there was a dearth of unconditional love, that's going to have a big effect. But even if you're fairly normal and balanced, that is, if you're from an average dysfunctional family, your life will change. And you'll change with it.

And when everyone you meet wants to be your friend, you can be friendly to everyone, but you can't be friends with everyone. Still, you do make new friends. But who makes the cut? Generally, we're inclined to develop friendships with people who make us feel good about ourselves, people who validate us. We go where we're accepted, admired, respected, and loved (unless you're really screwed up). When you feel loved you get a shot of dopamine in the brain and that feels pretty good. We go where the dopamine is.

But as a celeb, you get to meet very interesting people. And when a celebrity meets a Nobel prize winner, the President of the United States, a Beatle, a Governor, a Prime Minister, a Rolling Stone, a sports star, royalty, etc.—and they light up in your presence? You just made their day? You get an extra squirt of dopamine in the brain, and you bristle with warmth and happiness. It's not that the fame that goes to your head: it's the dopamine in your brain.

Which is not how Sandie would feel when she would see me. I never triggered some deep and luscious pleasure deep inside her. I knew her as a friend and a talented actress on the rise, and I treated her accordingly. But I didn't fawn. And even though she wasn't very comfortable with people fawning over her, when the President of the United States fawns over you, you can't help but react. You just get to meet more interesting people—interesting people who treat you like a star. Garcon! More dopamine!

I used to be on her party "A" list, but when you're a star? That list expands. You get moved down to the alternate "A" list, and eventually, after time, off that list completely. Displaced by people who are not more important, but they're more important because they are nicer to her.

I had two friends who were dating women on the rise. Their girlfriends were each noticed by an actor who shall go nameless (okay, it was Brad Pitt). And Mr. Pitt flirted with them and asked them out, but they had to decline. Why? Because they were in relationships. You think they wanted to be in relationships at that time? And when I say that time, I mean the second after Brad Pitt asked them out. No, they didn't. They wanted to be footless and fancy-free. Single. Available. Available for Brad Pitt. And so they broke up with their boyfriends and went out with Mr. Pitt.

And to some degree, that's what's going on. They're on the rise, and they want to grow and be unattached. And since their anonymity is irretrievably lost to the past, they want to control what little of their lives they still have left. The parts they can control. And sometimes that means moving on.

And sometimes it means moving away. Sure, your life is wonderfully graced—you get a VIP laminate to the world. To everywhere and everyone. When you walk into a room, a store, a restaurant, any place people light up. You made their day. And they just notice you. Some stare. If you laugh, they notice; if you're angry, they notice. You're being watched at all times. It's like being paranoid, except paranoia is when you think you're being watched when you really aren't. But they really are being watched. All the time. Which can be kinda creepy. Which is why some stars run off to live in a small town or build compounds to provide a little security and a semblance of privacy. And even if you have a compound, there could be someone parked outside. Waiting for you to leave. That's more than kinda creepy.

So even though I'm no longer on Sandie's "A" list (if she still has one), I suspect that if I ever run into her it'll be all hugs and kisses. And we might even re-kindle our friendship. But if we don't, it's fine. I still consider her a friend; we've just lost contact. And in fact, I believe she's moved away for reasons I don't know, but it wouldn't be hard to guess.

This is a town that provides a whirlwind of opportunity to fall from grace. And they are ready when you are. The paparazzi hang out at popular restaurants and any misstep will be recorded and disseminated within minutes. There are those that want you to fall and fail and will profit from your misery. So what's to lose by avoiding that? Not much, really. The best way to stay grounded is to find a place with actual ground. L.A.—if you're in the biz—is in the clouds and not that place, more a combo plate of Heaven and Hell.

In Los Angeles as well as in New York, there are plenty of little Satans trying to be your friend in exchange for providing access to anything—legal and otherwise. Note that kissing the hem of your garment and washing your feet in their tears often comes at a price, usually for a little piece of your soul.

Perhaps the alternate title of this book could be *A Guide Thru*

Hell. It could come in handy not just for celebrities but anyone who comes into quick money. I have some advice for you. And since Top 10 Lists are fun, here are 10 bits of advice for the New Celebrity.

1. All the attention makes you think this will last forever. It might, but the amount of stars who hit big and fall off soon are too many to mention. An actor can keep it going as long as their movies make money. No exceptions. Which brings us to the bottom line—#2.

2. It's all about money. Sure they'll tell you have talent, and you maybe you do, but it's really all about money. If you do your best work and it doesn't make money, you will fall quickly. And the moment you falter, their attention will be drawn to whatever is making more money. "They" are about as sophisticated as a virus that evolves to bind to a specific protein (actually the virus is more sophisticated). It's a very simple formula for them. Don't judge them too harshly. Just understand them for who they are. You can't train a shark to become a vegetarian. They eat meat. That's what they do. Accept it; just avoid becoming lunch. They'll eat you if there's a profit in it.

3. Invest your first big checks. Stocks can be risky, bonds less so. But a residential income property, AKA an apartment building, is your safest bet. Commercial property, rental homes, and second homes are vulnerable to recessionary forces. When that happens, stores close and are hard to rent. People who lose their homes will need a place to live and usually move to apartments. Buying

these buildings has been a pretty solid and stable formula. (Better return on your money if it's out of Los Angeles or out of state for that matter.) Do this and you'll have a reliable monthly check coming in every month for the rest of your life. And, with residential income, you can deduct the depreciation and the credit interest on the loan (you will make a down payment, get a loan, and the income will pay for the loan AND give you money to play with). Tax laws benefit landlords (and benefit oil investments). It adds up to sound and safe investments. Lease a car instead of buying, and you can deduct the lease payments.

4. Get a good accountant. He/she will explain the above stuff about deductions and will likely have similar investments. You can find them from a large, reputable and venerable firm. There are many stories about people who get ripped off by business managers. Some are old friends; some are family members. It just happened to one of my best friends a week ago. His manager took ALL of his money *and* a line of equity on his house. My friend is now broke AND in the hole. The FBI is involved, and he is wearing a wire to sting this guy. You don't want to do that, do you?

5. The business is rife with idiotic snake charmers. Their sole skill is charm. You can be friends with them, but you must always understand the dynamic. And if you must do a deal with them— get it in writing. (See 10a).

6. It is impossible to tell who your friends really are. Some will

always be your friends, but some get a touch of fame themselves and they're gone. It is amazing who will react this way. Someone you've known for decades, someone you've helped, might just drop you flat the moment they see an opening. It's hard to predict, and almost amusing when it happens. But it will contribute to your sense of cynicism.

7. Choose your projects wisely. Actors and singers are interpretative artists and only as good as the material they choose. Stumble once and you're on probation, but three strikes and you're out. You're no longer promising, and you've fallen from the pantheon. Sure, you'll make money doing movies that don't get released. But why be that person?

8. Agents and managers. Some are great; most are not. Trust no one implicitly. Be pro-active in your career. Bad agents or mismanagement destroys more careers than drugs, sex, bad marriages and bad reviews. How do you find them? Ask other, established artists. People who have been to Hell and back have maps and black books.

9. Your bosses. Understand that idiots are everywhere. Movies, TV, and Music execs by and large are not brilliant people. (If they had talent, they'd be talent.) Of that group, movie execs are least dumb, but they're still pretty dumb. TV is dumber, and music has the dumbest execs of all. There are exceptions. Find them; covet them.

10. Get a pre-nup! One of the great perks of Fame & Fortune is that you will suddenly be dating above your normal division. Caveat emptor! A good pre-nup is a solid investment. (see 10a)

    10a. Get a good lawyer. An attorney you can trust will be your friend for life.

    10b. Before you announce your divorce, meet with the top 10 divorce lawyers for one hour. When the hammer comes down and your spouse goes shopping for a lawyer, they won't be able to use any of those lawyers you met with and have to go with a "B" list lawyer.

11. Last piece of advice—buy this book! Read it! Study it! Repeat!

                              - Dale Launer, Screenwriter
                                My Cousin Vinny
                                Dirty Rotten Scoundrels
                                Ruthless People

Fame 101 is needed to teach people what's coming: the swell of people, requests, the letters, the e-mails, the greetings on the street, the honking of horns, the screaming of your name.
    – Giles and Rockwell, "Phenomenology of Fame"

Introduction

Some people laugh when I tell them I mentor celebrities and other high-profile achievers to help them navigate the unique challenges that come with fame. With thousands, if not millions of adoring fans, high salaries, a fabulous lifestyle, freebies, and opportunities, how could fame be burdensome? Truth is, celebrity can be both a blessing and a curse. Good fortune often brings pressure, demands, and unrealistic expectations. Celebrity is a kind of OZ. It's an alternate world a dragon called Fame lives and thrives on the broken souls it devours. To survive and thrive in this land, you need to tame the dragon. Furthermore, although your public image may take years to build, it only takes seconds to break—and forever to repair. Navigating these challenges requires a strong inner compass. In the rarified air of celebrity, I help my clients stay grounded, admired, inspired, and sane in an insane world.

Whether your fame is the result of a life-long pursuit or came to you by some sort of divine fate, where do you go from here? How do you successfully manage fame and deal with life when lived openly in the public arena? Some say you have to find ways to cope. Bollocks. Why cope? It's an exhausting and unfulfilling way to go. Wouldn't you rather thrive? The key is in your ability to maintain your authenticity, stay true to what you value most, understand boundaries, and know when, where and how to present yourself in a public forum.

I believe you are here in this life to be and to express the highest version of yourself. If you're an actor, successful entrepreneur, manager, agent, musician, high-profile executive, pro athlete, runway model, or reality show star, you know the questions you face in your personal and professional life:

- How do you stay grounded in a seemingly crazy world?
- How do you make consistent sound decisions no matter what?
- How do you leverage your high profile to make a unique, remarkable and uplifting impact?

In this book, I will share with you the lessons that I learned from my close encounters with the celebrated. Whether you're already in the spotlight, you aspire to achieve fame, or you work with celebrities, this book is for you. Through practical tips, real stories, and a tremendous amount of research and training, I will show you how to stay focused and grounded in the spirit within you so you'll know where to go and how to get there. You'll learn how to use your inner compass to guide you and show the way.

Success and recognition bring power. I've seen people cringe when I speak about power (as if the word is permanently packaged with an offensive attitude). Whenever I use the word "power," I'm referring to the innate ability to create positive or negative outcomes. That ability is in each and every one of us. Fame offers a significant infusion of energy and access to this natural human trait.

My interest in the effects of fame was awakened very early in life. Fame almost destroyed my family.

My father became supremely successful in his professional sphere. As one of the leading forensic neuropsychologists of his time, he became a highly sought-after public personality who was called upon to attend to high-profile cases. In the beginning, it was a pleasure to see him demonstrate his professional prowess with aplomb and without any airs of being affected by his accomplishments.

However, the recognition and the constant media attention were too good to resist. Without realizing it, he became a caricature of the person he really was, a victim of his own acts of entitlement and of the grandeur of his achievements. He started to believe his press. He fell prey to the notion that the public persona fame had crafted around him was indestructible and that alienated him from who he really was: a person who loved doing his best and who could be hurt if he failed. Fail he did-by being reduced to the definitions that fame bestowed upon him. Instead of being empowered, he became a victim.

I witnessed him self-sabotage his career on a very public stage, and in the bargain, he put his family and the people who cared for him through an intense public drama. I can still recall the shame and anger over what the media did, the outrage at the way in which our private lives were laid bare for all to see. The *Schadenfreude* of the same public who lauded his achievements reveled in his humiliation. For me, this experience revealed the fleeting nature of fame.

I could have been a victim of fame. Instead of allowing the harrowing experience to overcome my life, I chose to turn the very circumstances that influenced me negatively into the strength that could enable me to help others from succumbing to the vagaries of fame.

Ever since, I have made it my mission to objectively study how fame affects personality and perspective and how to make the most of it. The insights I share here are based on my own personal experiences and the wisdom I have gleaned by diligently studying how fame affects people. I've learned and observed how fame influences the famous as well as the people around them, including family members and close friends.

I took the experience and turned it into my mission to develop an acute understanding of fame that I can share with others to empower their own lives. My approach to fame is, therefore, based on a compassionate study and understanding of celebrity status. My judgment is not clouded by the aura surrounding celebrities because I can separate the smoke and mirrors from reality. I apply this objective approach to advise and coach celebrities, and those who aspire fame, to channel their energies in the right direction. This enables them to attain maximum leverage from the media attention to manage the life they deserve.

This book serves as a guide, a manual, a training course to provide you with the necessary tools and information to powerfully take on the rollercoaster of fame and enjoy the ride. It is born out of my early experiences, research, celebrity interviews, and-most importantly-discussions I've had with my many clients who've shared their insights and tips generously in support of those who follow in their footsteps. Honoring privacy and individual comfort, nearly all communication I have with a client is done over the phone. There are times when I'm asked to meet at someone's home, hotel, or on location. When I do, my client and I are the only ones in the room. Nothing is recorded. Conversations are held and notes are taken under a strict and fiercely protected confidentiality agreement.

While the book may be read cover-to-cover, the material is presented in a way that enables you to use it as a reference, turning to whatever section will serve you best in that moment. Like everything else in life, embrace what serves you. Take the note (especially the one that pisses you off). If you're "triggered," then that's a sign of something that wants attention and new direction. Put aside what doesn't ring true for you. Ultimately, you know what's best for you-the real you, the person behind the persona. I invite you to write in the margins. Add your own wisdom as you move forward as the steward of your fame and fortune.

Chapter One
Understanding Fame

If you ignore the dragon, it will eat you. If you try to confront the dragon it will overpower you. If you ride the dragon, you will take advantage of its might and power.

– Chinese proverb

There was no rulebook. There was nobody to navigate me through the experience of being watched all the time and nobody to tell me how to be normal when everybody is acting and looking at me differently.
 – *Leonardo DiCaprio*

For your consideration...

You've arrived. You got here by bus, by Bentley, by hook or by crook. No longer down and desperate, you're doing wonderfully well. You may not even want to be here but, like it or not, here you are. There's no turning back. Even if you turn your back on your notoriety, you can't return from whence you came. You're not the same person anymore. Fame has touched you and left an indelible impression.

Fame isn't quite what you expected, is it? There are plenty of advantages that automatically come with this level of achievement. Wherever you go, everyone likes you. You get lots of free stuff. People want to do things for you. You start to believe you really are special. To stay special, you'll have to learn how to effectively leverage your position to reach higher and grander vistas-without risking a fall.

You may have already experienced some of fame's perils.

- How long will my success last?
- Is this role the last one I'll every play?
- The last script that will get optioned?

The anxiety over when it will all end never goes away, no matter how many years you've worked steadily in your profession. You remain only as good as your last performance, and you realize you're still one engagement away from becoming a "has-been."

From the outside, your life looks like a charmed experience. From the inside, you feel conflicted, restless, uneasy. It feels weird to have strangers think they know (and own) you. The line starts to blur between who you really are and who you're expected to be. It's upsetting to read comments by reporters and fans that assume things about you that aren't true. You never expected to be seen as a fanciful object rather than a flesh and blood human being who can be hurt. And why do people, even those you know intimately, suddenly act differently in your presence?

How do you stay grounded, admired, inspired, and sane in a seemingly insane world? Now that you've achieved the goal for which you fought so hard, how do you keep the magic and excitement you felt when you first reached success? How are you to thrive, let alone endure? How do you encounter the dragon, face your fears, and stretch the limits of your potential without destroying yourself in the process?

The dragon is here to stay. It arrived long before you did and claimed its territory, and it will be here long after you're gone. Fame will never ever be loyal. It can turn on you quickly and with finality. What you can do is learn how to ride the dragon like a Blue Ribbon winner until its relatively tamed and follows your command.

Celebrity, Famous, or Star

I don't think I responded very well to the sudden
celebrity, the sudden fame and the loss of privacy.
– David Schwimmer

You can achieve fame through your talent, yet fame doesn't guarantee you a place at Celebrity's table. Because our modern language blurs the meaning of each word and an individual's status is fluid, shifting from one to the other or combining each category, I use the terms *famous, celebrity, star, talent, persona*, and *personality* synonymously throughout the book, though it is important to acknowledge their distinctions.

There may not seem to be much difference, and the terms *famous celebrity* and *star celebrity* are often interchangeably used. Understand that celebrity was originally used to refer to the condition of being famous. (One has to admit, when you look at it this way, it sounds a bit like an illness: a condition one has unwittingly caught or come down with.) It was only later used to refer to the person who is famous. Tracing the etymology of the word *celebrity* throws more light on what the word implies. It is derived from *celebrate*, which means to frequent, to solemnize with an Assembly of men; to honor by a great assembly. A celebrity, then, is the subject of solemn honor by the public. It is a position granted by consensus, and a state of being that is (being literal here) holy among men, those who are (again being literal) fanatical about your rise to the heavens. It is an honor, and if it is treated as such, you will be held in the highest esteem of your fans.

Even though these words are commonly used interchangeably, there are distinctions between them. A talented star is one who is known for an extraordinary ability. A famous person is renowned for the total of all people who've heard the person's name and can connect it with a face, voice, brand, or idea. A celebrity is a phenomenon created by a society that collectively cares about a person for reasons that outweigh or have little to do with their talent or merit. The differentiation can be seen when you consider Sir Richard Branson, the British business magnate and investor who's best known as the founder and chairman of Virgin Group of more than 400 companies. While Branson has fame and a very dynamic charismatic personality, very few people care where he dined last night or with whom.

Kim Kardashian, on the other hand, is one of the today's most-buzzed about celebrities. Her bio lists her as an American, one of the highest earning reality television personalities. Every aspect of her life is on display for those who feast at the buffet offered for those obsessed by all things Kardashian.

The first celebrities, like the Kardashians, were the powerful gods of the Greek and Roman pantheons. People of ancient civilizations believed the gods had a direct impact on their lives. Therefore, it was important to learn as much as you could about each god. Celebrity evolution soon came to Earth during that same period: monarchs, political leaders, and professional athletes began to make an impact on the populace. Victors in the ancient Olympic games were treated as mythic heroes, often elevated to god-like status. During the Renaissance, painters and sculptors began to realize a level of notoriety. These artists began to eclipse religious and political figures, a trend that continues today. This period also saw the rise of the "named" author, such as the 17th century playwright, poet laureate, and literary thinker Ben Jonson, who is best known for his satirical plays that gave him the status of the first "producer personality."

The expansion of celebrity accompanied the developing ideas about selfhood and individuality during the 18th century and gave rise to the inevitability of modern celebrities who embodied new ways of being in public, to be admired or emulated. The need for esteem drives our desire to be recognized for our individuality. We come to get a sense of famous and the celebrated at an early age. In the United States, celebrities are god-like royalty.

In the early 1900s, when print media extended into the film and radio, movie stars became the pinnacle of the A-list celebrities. Hollywood became Fame's capital. The rise of television solidified celebrity status as fame's faces were now seen every living room, bedroom, and (occasionally) bathroom. The rise of the Internet made global consumption of the minutiae of celebrity life within anyone's grasp in a few clicks of a mouse. It also brought the possibility of fame to the masses.

Not all celebrities are the same. Not all high-profile people pursued that status for the same reason. Fame is ephemeral, or at least it is in most cases. The driver of fame is often an urge to play an important role in the human drama of the day. Of course, there are many famous people who are no longer in our midst and yet they are still famous. We remember the work they did more than the person or how they looked or what clothes they wore. When you look at the telephone, do you recall the face of its inventor, Graham Bell? Or when you think of x-ray, does it conjure up an image of Marie Curie? Similarly when you watch Macbeth on stage or on screen, you don't remember what Shakespeare looked like, do you?

This state (akin to a sort of immortality or cult status) is the real thing. However, most types of fame do not last even a decade. In today's modern world, everyone has become extremely media-aware, but they also have a remarkably short attention span. So it seems Andy Warhol's much touted "15 Minutes" has been reduced a 15-second soundbite.

Included in today's hall of the famous and infamous are Reality TV stars, political figures, news and expert pundits, pro-athletes, authors, and high-profile criminals. In an ever- increasing plethora of content-rich media platforms that feed the diverse interests of society, there is unprecedented opportunity for the unknown to become known. Fame has become a goal to be achieved in a life narrative. The *everyday person* can now lay claim to cultural distinction and become part of the marketing machine that fuels the public's insatiable appetite for high-profile consumption. The masses measure their own yardstick of credibility based on their association with, or expertise in, celebrity culture.

Famous talk show doctors like Dr. Drew, Dr. Laura, and Dr. Phil are now more known for their celebrity than they are for their specialized skill. Top political pundits, including Sarah Palin, Jesse Jackson, and Andrew Weiner, are more known for their antics than their politics. Richard Branson, Steve Jobs, Larry Ellison, and Meg Whitman have realized the benefits and costs with the media-enhanced role of "Celebrity CEO."

To avoid the perils of overexposure, some authors now write under secret and not-so-secret pseudonyms in order to publish on their own merits without hype or expectation. J.K. Rowling writes under the pen name Robert Galbraith. Stephen King's *nom de plume* is Richard Bachman. Some authors leverage a celebrity name to create a cottage industry of books "written by" a famous name, though it's a team of ghostwriters who actually write the manuscript. James Patterson's 3-year, 17-book deal trades on his name, even though it is highly unlikely that any one person can crank out that many books in such a short time—at least not with any quality. What is a more likely, really, is that well-compensated "research assistants" are writing the prose. Many celebrities, including a plethora of public commentators like Glenn Beck and Bill O'Reilly, leverage their name to sell a lot of books that are written by hired ghostwriters.

Today, a famous personality or celebrity is instantly recognizable, thanks to the person's appearance in the media and the public's constant exposure to how they look, their obsession with the way they dress, the color and style of their hair and awareness of many other idiosyncrasies. Life's a crazy carnival when you find yourself caught up in a whirlwind of attention, much of it meaningless. Four hundred years ago, the most famous author in the English language summed up the full complexity of the relationship between celebrity and the media in a single line: "Life is a tale told by an idiot, full of sound and fury, signifying nothing." It hasn't changed much.

There are many paths to fame. It can be earned by working hard and smart, moving steadily and slowly along towards iconic status in your industry. You can be born into a famous family, winning a membership into the "lucky sperm club." Some embarrass their way to fame-and a boatload of money. A despicable deed will render you infamous. You can be touched by a stroke of luck, stumbling upon fame accidentally without any formal training or purposeful pursuit. Today, technology facilitates fame. Social networks fuel and propel the new cult of celebrity.

Reluctant and unwanted fame strikes those who find themselves in the cross-hairs of the wrong place/wrong time or misguided intention. Then there are those famous for being famous. If you're in that category and want to remain famous and respected, you must be able to back up your fame with smarts, ability, and a talent of some sort.

However you came to fame, unless you use your fame as a tool and put it to work for you, it will work against you, as many celebrities only realize too late. You should enjoy your fame rather than merely coping with it. Instead of being afraid of vilification, be positively expecting encouragement to do something enduring and for which you will be cherished and remembered.

Our world is a system of polarity. There is a good side as well as a bad side to fame. The allure of fame's fortune, public adoration, and preferential treatment can keep you stuck in a perpetual need to feed the dragon. Some say fame is the most relentless addiction. A common complaint about our celebrity culture is that the public has shifted from seeking the talents and virtues of the famous to seeking those who are most aggressive in self-promotion and who break ethical boundaries.

Lasting fame is about being a celebrity who cares about the larger world and who can grasp the magnificence of each day. Behave with a sense of respect and responsibility for the status that has been conferred on you. You deserve it, but remember it is not just something that you have achieved. It is also something that the community bestowed upon you. Unlike the authority granted within the religious and political doctrines of the Divine Right of Kings or the Mandate of Heaven, what is awarded can also be taken away. Celebrity doesn't come with an immutable divine right to reign supreme. It is entirely defined by your relationship to your audience.

Your being famous doesn't mean that you are infallible. You are (after all) human, just like everyone else. You are made of flesh and blood and prone to make mistakes. The public, however, tends to view people like you as super-human. As such, mistakes are unacceptable. Excellence is expected and, therefore, not a notable media event. That's why an actress winning an award isn't going to be the talk of the town or what the audience wants to hear-at least not much beyond the night of the award. The same actress doing something improper, be it misbehaving in public or making a fashion *faux pas*, is considered an epic media moment that, if mismanaged, can have legs that can walk for miles-until exhaustion derails the journey (and the career). The very same people who idolized you will rejoice in your fall. Fame has a heady effect when it treats you well, but it can be equally brutal when the tables are turned.

Modern Celebrity

You can take Elvis. You can take Marilyn Monroe.
Success and fame will not be the answer if something
inside of you is bothering you, if things in your mind
aren't going right.

—Linda Evans

We are witnessing a sea-change in the nature of what it means to be famous. The brilliant screenwriter who graciously wrote the foreword to this book and friend, Dale Launer, has been around the block of celebrity more than a few times. Based on what he's witnessed, he believes all stars are affected by fame. The issue is: by how much?

There are some celebrities who thrive on the fame and enjoy every minute of it. There are others who are not prepared for the invasion of privacy that inevitably must follow. The dragon we call fame has smote many. While the desire for recognition, to be seen, is a fundamental human need, fame is viewed as the ultimate form of a validated existence. The quest for fame unites a person's desire to be seen, heard, appreciated, and lauded others, the world, and himself.

Fame may bring fortune, yet wealth alone is insufficient to creating meaningful fame. Hungarian-American business magnate George Soros, billionaire industrialist David Koch, hotelier W. Barron Hilton, software entrepreneur Bill Gates, and investor Warren Buffett are famous for being really, really wealthy. What gives meaning to their celebrity isn't the wealth itself; it's what they and their families have done and contributed to with what they've earned that keeps their name in the cultural conversation. Money is tangible and clearly visible. Fame is intangible and mystical. At its root, the attraction to fame is in its perceived ability to satisfy the longing to be valued, appreciated, and desired by the community.

Once fame is achieved, what then do the famous want to be? Ironically, for many, they wish for a return to anonymity. Many want to be another nameless face in the crowd once more, with a new appreciation for the privacy the general public takes for granted. Yet, once the spotlight is focused upon you, there doesn't seem to be any respite from the all-seeing, critical, and relentless public adulation.

As Aviva Drescher, cast member of *Real Housewives of New York* and passionate philanthropist said to me, "If you're invited to the party, you have an obligation to participate. You have to engage. You have an obligation to your fans, the public, and the press to be graceful and elegant to the hand that feeds you." In order to do that, you have to see fame as a tremendous opportunity to do something that is meaningful to you in a much bigger way. It can't become a burden, a horrible beast that must be tolerated or fought.

Fame is often a byproduct of success. Yet very few came to fame and celebrity with the skills for managing fame, much less successfully thriving with their new-found status. There is a tendency to become self-absorbed and selfish as you receive more and more from others whose lives revolve around you and your needs and desires. Many have difficulty accepting rejection and failure because their very livelihood depends upon acceptance and success.

Stepping upon the platform of fame, you announce, "I've arrived." All your life you've been passionately driven to be the best at what you do. Dreaming. Planning. Practicing. Wishing. Aspiring. You now excel and people admire you for your prowess and your achievement.

Soon, though, you recognize lasting fame isn't easy. The days of being able to develop your public image quietly are gone. The struggle with dealing with fame is now entertainment for others, a sporting event for the fever frenzied, celebrity-obsessed crowds.

Modern day celebrity is the ultimate reality programming. The phenomenon embraces the global conversation about anyone who is known for his *well-knownness*. The narrative can be either good or bad. The awareness may be substantial in merit or hollow. Greatness of achievement is optional. Fame can evolve naturally or be cleverly and creatively manufactured. With the rise of Spice Girl celebrity where the high-ranking band was assembled like a machine with interchangeable parts, lots of rehearsal and brilliant branding the phenomenon has elevated to an art form in itself.

To be a celebrity today requires maintaining a consistent presence as a subject in the narrative of society. The media and its consumer populace have a front row seat to the movie that is your life. The plot doesn't need to be well developed. If it includes crowd-pleasing *sexcapades* or a runaway temper tantrum, all the better. Your stunned realization is that there is suddenly more emphasis on your chronicle than your extraordinary capability.

This doesn't mean that those who've achieved their way to fame aren't relevant. They are. Exceptional qualities or capabilities are always a good tale and serve as a foundation for the ongoing biographical essay of our culture. However, these attributes aren't essential to sustain one's celebrity. It's quite possible to skip the laborious undertaking and go straight for the buzz. If this is your adventure, it is prudent to travel it wisely, fully equipped, and with a well-lit and well-mapped path. That would be quite an achievement indeed. Regularly broadcast your role in the narrative beyond a forgotten footnote or a one-shot anecdote. If you do this and remain interesting and relevant, you can claim your celebrity status was well earned.

If you don't want to be a victim of the fame hangover, then don't succumb to the unrealistic demands and expectations it places on you. Keep evolving. Like a well-told story, craft a compelling beginning, engaging middle, and meaningful end. Be congruent and positively rooted in your character development. Consider celebrity as an art and a process, not a singular event. Put fame in its place beside you instead of above of you.

Fame is an evolution of transition that goes through several stages of change from one condition to another. Like the stages of growth and grief, celebrity is largely a developmental process that can both weigh heavily upon and invigorate the emotional soul. While the show of fame outwardly expresses progress, the real advancement is achieved through the strengthening of your inner core. The heartbreak or fulfillment of fame's promise can only be experienced from within. Through each graduating phase, the pitfalls of celebrity fade as its potential begiens to flourish.

The Four Stages of Fame

Fame hit me like a ton of bricks.
– Eminem

Are you moving ahead or going around in circles? Whether you aspire to or already have achieved celebrity status, it's time to introduce you to the four stages of fame. The Giles and Rockwell report, Phenomenology of Fame, first introduced a staged view of the fame experience. I've shifted and expanded their initial concept based on my own research and client experience. You may have already experienced one or more of the following stages of fame:

1. *The Honeymoon*
2. *Dependency*
3. *Acceptance and Adaption*
4. *Empowered*

The Honeymoon

I've always been famous, it's just no one knew it yet.
– Lady Gaga

In this first stage, you love your newfound status. So do your fans. This is the honeymoon period, when you can do no wrong. Fame is fun. You love it. There is something magical about feeling the unrequited love of millions of strangers. Sometimes you hate it, but you fall quickly in love again.

As a celebrity, to be a part of the celebrations is initially a wonderful experience. It is something you fall in love with. You suddenly become aware of the adulation of your fans. You have a sense of belonging but you become aware that you have a role to play, a duty to fulfill, so as to live up to your fan's expectations.

The prestige and the privileges that fame brings can be empowering. Doors open without you realizing it. People acknowledge your presence wherever you go. You feel great. Fame and fortune raises you from the plane where problems and obstacles abound to a level where the going is smooth, everyone you meet is wonderful, and things happen faster and easier than you ever thought possible.

Things are going so well that it is too good to be true. You start to think that it has to turn sour-and it does. Sooner or later, you find that what was initially a joyride turns into a roller coaster, and it's going out of control. If the constant in-your-face attention of the paparazzi doesn't get to you first then once benevolent "watchful eye" of the main-stream media starts waiting for you to slip up. It could be an unflattering picture that caught you unawares or a quote wrongly attributed to you. You try to stifle your scream because you didn't do anything to deserve this negative feedback loop. Why don't they leave you alone?

The loss of privacy and loss of freedom that a deluge of attention can bring can change your perspective and the way you behave. It is natural for you to wish for anonymity, especially when you want a respite from the constant barrage of attention and need some "me-time" to recoup and recover from the early stages of being famous.

Danger lurks. The pressure, demands, and expectations can get to you. All of a sudden, you find yourself triggered, behaving in an unexpected manner in public in ways that really aren't "you." The constant scrutiny belies your truth. Your career can quickly change if what you do or say is detrimental to how your fans perceive you. Even the small things become monumental. Everyone has "bad hair days." As a celebrity, you've lost the privilege of experiencing those days in private. Your falls from grace are broadcasted as "falls from grace." They are printed Tweeted, YouTubed, socially networked, and world-wide-webbed into a virtual frenzy that can sideline key events on a national stage. Ridiculous, I know. Yet you see it happen to good-hearted people like you. Every day.

When you see yourself surrounded by mirrors, it's only a matter of time before the illusion shatters. Everywhere you look, you see your public image reflected in people's eyes and in their demeanor. The glow of honeymoon starts to wane. You think that you've had enough, but it's only the beginning. You still have desires and ambitions. You exercise these feelings and act on them. Your daily interactions may seem innocuous enough to you but your fans are closely watching you. You want to be the person you really are. But that image may not coincide with the person that your fans wish you to be. This is where the conflict arises. It's challenging enough to learn how to be comfortable in one's own skin, let alone have to balance that with some sort of media-acceptable persona that has become your public image. Living a fabricated life centered within a false value, where your life is to be played out like a character in a movie, breeds discontentment and is impossible to sustain. Yet star power depends on the keeping the media interested, and the media's survival depends upon sating the public hunger for celebrity private news and information. Fame is risky. It can be a triple-edged sword, where there is your side, the media's side, and the truth. The ambiguity and tension that arise eventually take their toll, usually expressed in poor decisions and bad behavior.

Paradoxically, if you navigate your way through the honeymoon phase of fame successfully you enter into phase two: Dependency. The ups and downs between the love/hate honeymoon experiences of phase one can lead to an addiction to fame, where you'll do whatever it takes-and risk making many misguided choices-to spend your time wrapped in the "high" of fame rather than its lows.

Dependency

Just cause you got the monkey off your back doesn't mean the circus has left town.
– George Carlin

Fame is enjoyable. Fame is addictive. Fame is a test of endurance.

At this stage you've become dependent upon your notoriety. Just like any good thing, indulging in too much of it can be a bad thing. Fame is like eating or drinking. You can be an epicure, a gourmet, and a connoisseur who appreciates good food, fine wine, and knows how to pick and choose.

On the other hand, you could be a glutton who never has enough. In one case, you are consciously seeking enjoyment; on the other, you don't know what you're seeking because the satisfaction you seek is beyond limitation and it will only hurt you end the end.

Enjoyment is found when you utilize your power and freedom to decide when and where to draw the line. Otherwise, what was once pleasurable becomes a compulsion that you hate yet can't give up. It becomes an *addiction*. This is what differentiates the workaholic from a passionate artist, the fame monger from the really famous.

In the second phase of fame it's easy to become hooked. The more you're loved and adored, the more you want that warm embrace, and the more afraid you become of losing it. The chill of its fleeting affection feels like a personal rejection. It becomes a ping-ponged existence where you bounce back and forth as you move away from pain towards pleasure and back into pain. The pleasures turn toxic.

The need for unwavering praise and validation, left unchecked, becomes perceived as a need, a bottomless void always needing to be filled. The illusion belies a healthy sense of self. If you are insecure in your own worth, you will do anything and everything to keep center stage in the proscenium of public awareness. While the media may be leveraged to create an intimacy with fans by revealing "normal" human everyday behavior, at the same time the public still expects larger-than-life social position and lifestyle. In an effort to deal with and keep up with unrealistic expectations, misguided choices will be made. Justifications will be created for poor results. Coping is stressful. When under stress, rational thinking gives way to irrational reasoning. Actions taken and behavior exposed in such a state can include taking offense or becoming angry over a situation that hasn't occurred, expressing exaggerated emotions, maintaining unrealistic expectations, irresponsible conduct such as intoxication, disorganization, or extravagance. It is at these times when celebrities are most vulnerable to confidence schemes, where they are easily defrauded by those who gain their trust in order to exploit their character and/or assets.

It's important to note that many who seem to be willing to do or say anything to remain in the public eye see fame as the magic wand that will cure an inner pain. What many view as narcissism is really a reflection of self-loathing. In a misguided effort to feel good about yourself and circumstance you will say and do anything-sometimes to the extremes-to place other people and things below you in order to feel better about yourself. When you see a person, celebrity or not, verbally beating on others, it's really a reflection of how badly they beat upon themselves through their inner dialog and the circumstances they create. It's a cry for help. It's the outer expression of the pain of the loss of a sense of esteem, love, belonging, and connection.

Being dependent on the constant confirmation of your value is a precarious way to live. There is great fear in falling out of favor. Cultivating an entourage to constantly affirm your significance, attractiveness, and brilliance devalues your self-worth and insulates you from a *healthy* ego. People you pay may be very friendly. Make no mistake: they are not your friends. They are there to be paid to do your bidding-whatever that may be. Often, they have a personal agenda (perhaps to grab their own claim to fame through their association with you). Co-dependent relationships are not healthy and often have bitter ends.

You'll find the flavor of the moment keeps changing because people desire new forms of excitement to remain entertained and engrossed. Being the same kind caricature, offering the same-old-same-old, may make you stale. Fans will look elsewhere to find whatever stimulus they are looking for. While remaining true to who you are, **evolve**. That evolution will be documented and publicized, enriching the layers that keep your audience interested and engaged.

Moving forward requires conscious balance. Too much time

away from the public eye and you could be forgotten. No one wants to be viewed as a has-been. Maintain a harmony of private and public moments. Life is never equally balanced. Time spent in and out of the public eye is best viewed as a harmonic dance between you and the spotlight.

The truth is, if you aren't able to give yourself—your true self—the attention, acknowledgement, and validation you crave, then no amount of fame will soothe your aching soul. The sooner you define your value from the inside, the sooner you'll be able to make the transition to the next phase, and direct your experience going forward.

Some individuals get stuck in this stage, never able to release fame's needy, clingy grip. In an existence of "more will always be better," the joy and inner peace, satisfaction and fulfillment with always be elusive.

Acceptance and Adaption

I believe you make your day. You make your life. So much of it is all perception, and this is the form that I built for myself. I have to accept it and work within those compounds, and it's up to me.

–Brad Pitt

In order to manage your fame and not let it derail your personal or public life, you need to accept fame in its entirety-the good, bad, and just plain weird. Condition yourself to the changes that are happening around you and within you. Be bullshit free. Be grounded. Be human. Be real. When looking for the tree of truth in a forest of illusions, the only reliable compass is your soul.

Actor Robert Pattison spoke to Spanish GQ magazine about what his life was like now that he was a movie star. Pattison responded, "It's strange, you don't have a normal life anymore. You spend much time trying to fight it, but in the end you find another way to live." You find a way to live with fame that works for you. Fame isn't a normal existence, so it's futile to wish it was. Fighting the dragon of fame will only enrage it. Make peace. Tame it so it can walk by your side as your friend.

You'll make mistakes. It's ok and it's normal. To err is human, after all. Growth is often a process of trial and error. Make growth part of your personal life and public persona. When you screw up, sit on your own bottom and own your mistake. Leverage your mistakes by becoming an example of positive change. No one is perfect. And why would anyone want to live with no room to learn and grow? Expecting perfection-of yourself and others-is a bullet train ticket to the land of disappointment and failure.

Acceptance is about being self-aware and self-directed enough to know your greatest (and not-so-great) qualities. Improve what you can, where you can, when you can. Turn the problem areas into positive opportunity. It takes a bit of self-reflection and a healthy dose of accountability. This is the secret sauce that will keep you from becoming one of the crisis-ridden people you see in the media today. When you can accept the whole of you and your circumstance, what you'll get in return is a profound sense of freedom, power, and peace. Life is a patient teacher. You know you've learned the lesson when it stops showing up in the classroom of your days.

The important thing is to be seen as someone who grows and

changes instead of someone who repeats the same mistake over and over again like a blind hamster on a treadmill. We all love a good story of a lesson learned well. While some celebrities remain relevant for the headlines-reporting a timeline of trouble-the public grows weary of someone in the public eye only for his or her transgressions, especially when the pattern repeats itself so much it's become the only thing they can remember about the former star.

Our experience is a constant flow of change. The ancient Greek philosopher Heroditous famously said, "You can't step in the same river twice." This is true of you, your image, and your public. How you are perceived, the moment of who you are in your life, constantly changes. You change, you make changes, and circumstances change. Prepare for change in order to keep moving forward. It's foolhardy to think that things can go back to the way they were before you became famous. No one can go back to that moment in time-and why, really, would anyone want to? Any growth, learning, achievement, or opportunity from that moment forward would be forfeited. And, like treading water, it'd get exhausting (and boring). So forget about what once was. It was never meant to remain anyway. In the adaption phase, your focus is turned upon how you can leverage, rather than merely tolerate, where you are.

Remember what was said earlier: be careful what you wish for, you might just get it. I'll add a layer to that piece of advice. As you wish, hope, and dream, get specific. If fame is your wish, get specific in your vision of what you want that experience to be like. Imagine how you'll positively manage your newfound status. If you're already famous, think of how you'd like your experience to evolve from this point on. You have the power to create that very experience-unless you get in your own way.

Remember, the events of your life are not the same as your experience. How you experience the events of your life is based upon the meanings you give it and that is shaped by your inner dialog. If you don't like an aspect of your situation, reach for a better perspective. You can't always shape reality, but you can shape how you handle the encounter. If it's downright awful, embrace its gift in the lesson that can be learned. Apply the lesson. Rinse and repeat. Otherwise, the most you can achieve is mediocrity. Mediocrity is meant to wallow in the shadows. That's not what you were born to do. To fritter away your talent and your fortune or to stay on the sidelines just because you choose not to find a way to adapt is a waste of your time and energy.

Realize there's a very thin line that separates reality from make-believe. There are fictional characters from movies or novels that seem more real than the people around us. That's because we tend to make a deeper connection with them. Similarly, some people idolize their heroes. It could be a football player, a singer, an actor, or a rock star. A poster on the bedroom wall comes to life in the imagination of a fan in the privacy of her life. It is human nature to be influenced by your connections.

Part of accepting fame is accepting the responsibility that comes with your influence. With the ability to make an impact comes a responsibility to set an example that is worthy of being followed. You have an opportunity to influence the lives of people, including impressionable young minds, to make this world a better place-or at least follow in your footsteps meaningfully. Shoulder this responsibility as a blessing instead of as a nuisance that prevents you from doing normal things that normal people do, such as walking on the beach without being photographed or going to a cafe without being accosted or stared at. You can still maintain your personal boundaries while sharing your light with those who help shine it upon you.

Fame, and all that comes with it, is now a part of your life but only a part. It's not your whole life. There is a larger part of your life as a famous personality that involves finding the time and the focus to continue doing the good work that made you famous in the first place. Once you realize this, you will start moving from *coping* with your celebrity status to *thriving* on it.

Adapt. The chameleon does not try to change its surroundings. It changes itself to fit its surroundings. It's a survival response, pure and natural. As the influential Persian poet Rumi once said, "Yesterday I was clever, so I wanted to change the world. Today I am wise, so I am changing myself."

It's kind of like playing a video game. Even if you don't pay attention and learn from your mistakes, you may continue playing but that doesn't mean that you are going to the next level. If you're outclassed or playing an unwinnable game, you need to get a grip on that reality. If you have decided to go with the flow, then you better stop and take a look around you. Does everything look very familiar? Do you keep getting a sense of déjà vu?

Knowing what to expect and staying insulated from the effects of being a celebrity will enable you to rise above the petty travails that fame takes you through. Going through the four phases of fame is inevitable. Being *prepared* will make it less of an ordeal, and you will be able to emerge the wiser.

The second and third phases of fame present a tug of war between the public persona and the private persona. Some people are good at compartmentalizing their public and private lives. However, this is not always possible, especially when you are incessantly being followed by the paparazzi. (We'll talk more about how to handle the paparazzi in a later chapter.) For now, let's move on to the final phase of a fame story well told: empowerment.

Empowered

> *Life is very interesting. In the end, some of your greatest pains become your greatest strengths.*
> – Drew Barrymore

The last stage is the realization of your full potential by leveraging fame's power. This is the stage where you leverage your fame and fortune to achieve a purpose profoundly meaningful to you. A significant part of being famous and fulfilled is the ability to consistently align yourself-your language, behavior and choices-with what you value most. As you evolve, there is a certain amount of re-invention or keeping it fresh, so that your work and your status as a role model are relevant to the changing times. But this change must come from the inside out. Ultimately, you'll feel enriched and autonomous in the four pillars of the human foundation: physical, mental, emotional, and spiritual.

Money, power, and fame are merely tools to make an enduring impact. Purpose, passion, and humility are what feed the soul of contentment and what makes sense out of this complicated world. The ability to stand for something beyond you is essential to the mission. Your fame, after all, was created of and beyond you. It took talent, perseverance, a touch of good fortune, and the random collision of savvy people and brilliant ideas. Now it's your turn to pay it forward.

Ask yourself: "Who do I want to become beyond my fame?" Yesterday's nobody is tomorrow's celebrity. Today's celebrity could be tomorrow's nobody. This is the classic "Wheel of Fortune" and is a fundamental tenant of the human condition. Like the tip of your nose, it's hard to see unless someone puts up a mirror. Then it's clear in the reflection. The ups and down of fortune is hard to recognize when you're spinning around. It is best viewed from a distance. The possibility of being no longer relevant is something that every celebrity has to face, accept, or overcome. The question becomes, then, how do you wish to be remembered?

I guarantee you that on your last day of life, if you're at all conscious, you won't be thinking about your fame or your fortune. You'll be reflecting upon the life you've lived and you'll wonder: "Did I matter? Did I make a difference for the people I love? In the world?"

If you haven't already, cultivate your personal passionate purpose. Passion makes sense out of this complicated world. A meaningful intention pursued with intense enthusiasm, dedication, and interest will give you the greatest personal return on your high-profile cachet. Your life's imprint is beyond any award, performance, credit, or title.

Actor Joseph Gordon-Levitt starting acting at age 6. He became famous playing an adult alien stuck in a human teenager's body in the popular television show *3rd Rock from the Sun*. Even as a young adult, he kept his feet firmly on the ground as he poured all of his energy into honing and evolving his craft. In his early twenties, he was confident enough to take a break from acting to attend Columbia University to study history, literature, and French poetry. Self-empowered early on, Gordon-Levitt never conformed to peer pressure or lived up to anyone else's expectations.

As one of Hollywood's biggest young stars, he stays true to his priorities: excellence, quality, and the work ethic required to achieve his unique status. Comfortable in his own skin, he comes across in interviews as a modest, affable down-to-earth guy. In a celebrity profile, he told GQ's Amy Wallace, "I really don't like this notion that some people are more important than other people. These stories about these elevated people called 'celebrities' teaches you"—and by "you," he meant regular people without fame—"that what you have to say doesn't matter. It's degrading."

Fame doesn't empower Gordon-Levitt. He empowers his fame. He maintains his balance while challenging himself to find new opportunities to improve. Keeping on top of our rapidly evolving time, he invested $500,000 in hitRECord.org, a website that is "an 'open collaborative production company' where people can make things together." One collaborative project was called Tiny Stories, where Gordon-Levitt told his own story about a childhood aspiration. The story was simple: "When I was younger, I wanted to be something. Now I just want to be younger."

Empowered fame is about appreciating where you are, what you have and what you get to do. It's about leveraging all of its potential to serve the greater good of all, including yourself. It's about realizing that fame, in and of itself, isn't a meaningful achievement. It's what you do with your fame that spotlights your character and lasts beyond your lifetime.

The Shadow of Fame

Most of the shadows in life are caused by our standing in our own sunshine.

– Ralph Waldo Emerson

You know who you are. You don't have to bother what your shadow is doing because it is just a reflection or an image of your authentic self. Just as your shadow needs you, your public persona needs your authentic self. Not the other way round. In Plato's "Allegory of the Cave," he describes a vision of people who are imprisoned in a cave since childhood, chained and faced with a blank wall. Puppeteers who stand in front of a fire behind the prisoners project shadows on the wall. According to Plato, these shadow representations are the closest these people get to their ability to see reality. They know nothing about the real cause of the shadows. Their beliefs and language are based merely on vague representations of what they think is real rather than what is actually real. In order to see what is real, the prisoners have to turn their heads and look at things from a different perspective— one that is real rather than an incomplete reflection. They have to get out of the cave. It is hard and uncomfortable at first, but once they see reality, the misleading shadows of the cave are easy to spot. Fame, like light, has a way of playing tricks on one's perception. Your shadow may seem bigger than you—depending on how you look at it. However, your shadow is always changing.

So is your public image. It's changing all the time. So, instead of attending to your authentic self, if you keep following your public persona, you are bound to lose your sense of perspective. That's when you get sloppy, trip, and fall. The media has a field day because you weren't watching where you were going. Instead, you were looking at your shadow and losing sight of your self.

Tower over your shadow rather than live within it. Live as what you value most and explore your deepest passions instead of living in the mask of your public persona. That's how you became famous in the first place: through cultivating your passion and following your instincts. By all means, pay attention to the narrative that is circulating about you. You can't ignore it. The more rumor is disseminated the more believable it gets. But…

- Listen to the stories without attachment. Otherwise, you are liable to lose your own self and what remains is just shadow, a public persona.

- Life isn't a fairy tale. A happy ending isn't guaranteed.

- Knights in shining armor can save the day.

- They can also fail to arrive or trample you.

- Peter Pan lost his shadow. It took someone to truly believe in him to help him find it again.

- True friends and close family cannot be overvalued.

Ultimately losing your true self is a bigger problem than losing your shadow. The disconnection from who you really are creates the despair in Henry David Thoreau's quote: "The masses of men (and women) lead lives of quiet desperation and go to the grave with the song still in them."

Fame is a journey, not a destination. There are many cautionary tales to be told along the way. In it, you can't put the pieces of your life together with the same approach as your career. Satisfying fame can't be forced. It doesn't arrive on schedule. When it finally shows up, take the time to take the edge off its newness. When you devour the fame too fast, like overeating, you aren't in a position to know when you're full (plus, you can't savor the meal).

With patience, you will stay out of your own way. Resist the temptation to make big decisions to quickly fix parts of your life that aren't the way you want it. If you've worked for years to earn enough money to have a relationship, home, and family, don't run out and acquire them as if you were on a race to catch up to whatever it is you think you've missed. It takes years to become successful. Allow yourself the time to succeed in the other areas of your life. Impulsive decisions are costly and often regretted. Move too fast and you may find yourself saddled with a divorce, the sale of your home and shared custody.

As you travel down the yellow-brick-road of fame, you may feel compelled to keep your sunglasses on at all times. There's a sadness that happens when you realize that people look at you like you are not really you. Shying away from how people look at you differently, you may not want to make eye contact with anyone. Doing so will only make you feel isolated, disconnected from the fabric of everyday life. Clients tell me they feel uncomfortable when fans, strangers, and friends give them *the look*. As if not human or larger than life people can hardly contain themselves in your presence. They forget how to talk, abandon basic manners, or stand frozen like a deer caught in the headlights as they give you a prolonged wide-eyed stare.

You can't change how the public deals with meeting you in person. All you can do is shift how you respond to their reaction. Take a tip from Gandhi. Be the change you wish to see. Take off your sunglasses, look the person straight in the eye, and engage with authentic confidence, compassion and consideration. No one does this better than Tom Hanks. He will often walk up to people, even those who stare at him with palpable awe and wonder and simply say, "Hi, I'm Tom." Audiences love him and speak of him as kind, gracious, and honest.

It's helpful to keep up the old routines that kept you in focused as you built your career. Many of my clients maintain a practice of meditation, yoga, spirituality, or other hobbies to keep them comfortable in their own skin. Learn from the people around you. Give yourself the advantage by learning their lessons without having to go through the pain of their experience. Consider the fulfillment of your potential as a contribution to something bigger. If you were in a position to help or provide leadership to others, what would you do? Are you doing that today? Why not? You wouldn't be where you are today without some support along the way. You know what it's like to need other people to give back. Now it's your turn. The satisfaction that comes with paying it forward will serve to continue to fuel your drive when the going gets tough.

It's a strange new world, clearly. That doesn't mean it isn't navigable. There are many who know the terrain well. Seek their sage advice and mentorship. Your innate intuition will serve as your ruby slippers or rugged boots to always help guide you in the right direction. Prepare yourself for an extraordinary adventure as magical as OZ.

Chapter Two
Navigating Fame

Like everybody in show business, you think you're going to wake up one day, and it's all going to be taken away from you. I think we all share an insecurity in that way, everybody in show business-the one's I talk to anyway.

– Rod Stewart

I think if you live in a black-and-white world, you're gonna suffer a lot. I used to be like that. But I don't believe that anymore.

– Bradley Cooper

I like to hide behind the characters I play. Despite the public perception, I'm a very private person who has a hard time with the fame thing.

– Angelina Jolie

Your Comfort Zone is Back There Somewhere

No matter how you arrived at your elevated profile, you begin to realize you've left your comfort zone. No matter how you envisioned your life after your public debut, the realities unfolding before you are quite different. You feel like a stranger in a strange land. If you think about it, this is how you came into the world. Suddenly you were thrust out of the comfort of the womb into an unfamiliar and unrecognizable world. You didn't even know how to articulate your needs and wants. Yet you managed to do at least a decent job of figuring it out as you grew. If you did it once, you can do it again. Be open and willing to trust that you would not be on this journey if you did not have the resources you need within you. You can choose to wisely navigate the unknown. You will be presented with difficult challenges and hurdles that will test you in all kinds of ways. Your skills will be tested. Your illusions will be dispelled. You will stumble and fall. Your fears and doubts will resurface. Temptations will arise that may lure you to abandon your call. So show up, fully present to the opportunity. Press on and continue to rise to the occasion, and your victories will be celebrated. In the process, you will develop a new and greater insight into your character, potential, and resilience.

Know the Territory

*Sure, I suffered a lot. But it's not like the end of the
world and its not who I am. I lead quite a pleasant
life and I'm able to divorce a perceived reality from
my actual experience of life.*

– Ben Affleck

Riding the dragon of fame not unlike a spiritual journey where the
conventional tools of charting a course in the physical world—such
as a roadmap or compass—are not enough. You need to develop your
own innate sense of direction to make sure you are connected with
your true character while being objectively aware of your behavior
as a public persona. The devil is in the details of what and how you're
willing to see. The territory to navigate is really the map of your mind
as much as it is the landscape of notoriety.

If fame is a game, make sure you know how it's played. It takes
a strong inner compass to navigate through the unique challenges of
fame and fortune. A lot of what you face won't seem fair—and it isn't.
Still, you'll have to deal with issues like the invasion of your privacy,
false accusations reported as news, and possible "bling ring" style
home invasions. You'll have incredible opportunities, meet some of
the most interesting people of your time, and live an enviable life. Yet
there will be days were you feel like it's "me against the world."

Once fame shines her light upon you, life as you knew it is over.
The change in your status can hit you like a tornado, and it can be just
as fast and destructive. They can also randomly pick you up and put
you down someplace you didn't expect. You're not in Kansas anymore,
as they say, and you feel out of control, powerless. What happened to

fame's promise?

It's there. Truth is, it always was. You didn't need fame to deliver power to you. You were born empowered. I'm not saying you can control everything in your life (no one can), but you can control how you react to the situation around you. Turn your focus to ways in which you can direct your life and your career. That's where the real power resides. In the following pages, you will learn how to direct your path, champion your destination, and triumph over tribulation. All you have to do is be willing, ready, and available for what comes next.

In many ways, fame is a contest where you compete with yourself. You will always win, but which you: the best or the worst version of yourself? Will your needy ego become aggrandized as it makes its claim to the world that it's winning? Or will your highest self, the part of you that's made up of your dreams, inspirations, and talents, be victorious? Since you are the only player, the outcome is entirely up to you. Make fame your friend instead of your master by becoming an awake, aware, and astute guardian of its prolific treasure.

It's important to orient yourself physically and spiritually to the new ground beneath your feet. Take time to observe, listen, and reflect as you enter the world of objectification, where real human beings can become formatted characters. With appreciation, say goodbye to the parts of your old life that must be left behind and hello to the new parts being birthed as a consequence of your expansion.

I'm assuming you already have a keen intellect. It helped to get you to where you are today. Keep its crucial companion, emotional intelligence, healthy and available to you at all times. Orient yourself and act towards your goal instead of unnecessarily holding on to the past. Be mindful of the inner dialog, attachments, and assumptions that block your fascinating journey. Recognize and monitor your change-resistant impulses (as well as your reckless impulses towards extremes) as you negotiate your newfound distinction. All the while, stay in touch with the voice in your heart that will remind you how to return to the embodiment of your true spirit. If you wander astray, that voice will lead you back to who you truly are.

Fame is transient. It doesn't last forever—at least not in the way you experience it. How short or how long it endures depends on how you choose to steer your fame. You could be famous for what you do best right now. Tomorrow, you could be famous for what you do best later on, which could be an altogether different thing. You've seen many celebrities start as an actor, a singer, or a sportsperson and become something else as their careers progress. They become champions for a social cause, successful entrepreneurs, and businesspeople. A few even managed to become mayors, congresspersons, senators, or the president of the country.

It's possible that one can be good at more than one thing. People will grant you recognition and respect for your many accomplishments apart from that one skill for which you are now famous. As long as you are doing something and are reasonably good at it, people will love you. It's when you fail at your additional pursuits and continue doing it without any growth: that's when public adoration turns to ridicule.

The masses, including the media, express the daily duality of their relationship with individual celebrities and the frenzy of fame. While the public gives rise to fame it can tear it down in an instant by systematically degrading a star's status. Some stars strip themselves of the reputation they've worked so hard to achieve misguided in their ability to cope with the real or unrealistic expectations that come with their pedestal position.

Fame is truly a paradoxical phenomenon. It's brilliance calls to many who through passionate dedicated work, an unexpected event or incredible luck suddenly find themselves face-to-face with the pressure and perils that come with their good fortune. When it comes to dealing with the business of celebrity and managing fame, your emotional intelligence (EQ) matters more than your intellect (IQ). The level of your EQ is evidenced by your ability to monitor your own and other's feelings and emotions, to discern between them, and to use this information to guide your thinking and actions for positive results.

It's grand to be acknowledged and validated. There is, perhaps, no greater feeling. It's a thrill to be admired and adored. The basic human need of a sense of love, belonging and connection is overwhelmingly fulfilled. How effectively you go about attaining and maintaining that sense of wellbeing is informed by your EQ, not your IQ.

Like the cup that runneth over, the 'high' of the onset of fame can quickly dribble back down to the ground drenching the warmth of the glow almost as quickly as it appeared. The shift from a love relationship with fame to a hateful relationship sometimes begins when you realize it's impossible to live up to the hype, the sparking image of your public persona. Deep within you feel like an impostor or know that it's only a matter of time before you'll disappoint that image. I'm really not who they think I am thoughts dim the light that came with the sense of love, belonging and connection.

When you and your life become talked about, you are at the mercy of those who tell the story: the media and the fans. In this business, you have to have a thick skin. It can be quite scary and risky to try to maintain a positive public image when every word spoken and every action taken can work against you. Mistakes aren't tolerated. Anything taken out of context seems "fair game." The Jekyll-Hyde attention takes on a *Schadenfreude*[1] tone where the very people who built you up work as avidly to tear you down.

The public seems to love you for what you've done and what you have, and they also hate you for doing it and having it. Even more daunting is the steady, watchful of the media. It has expanded exponentially now that anyone and everyone with a cell phone camera can become a paparazzo, Tweeting and sharing your 'bad hair' moments virally with their friends and friends of friends.

The paradox of your fame is that it gives you a resource to change your own life and the lives of others. It gives you the power to influence trends and control situations while also rendering you powerless when fame and the broad craving to be in the limelight overshadows your emotional and intellectual faculties. The emotional *dis-ease* exhibited by high-profile personalities in trouble is often misinterpreted as a designer label mental illness.

The total loss of privacy can take its toll. Harrison Ford describes this loss as an "incalculable cost."

> *You always think, 'If I'm successful, I'll have opportunities.' You never figure the cost of fame will*

[1] The direct English translation of the German word "*Schadenfreude*" is "damage-joy" or "fail-joy." *Schadenfreude* is a phenomenon when one is pleasured by the misfortunes of others or feels joy when seeing another fail.

be a total loss of privacy. That's incalculable. What a
burden that is for anybody. It was unanticipated and
I've never enjoyed it.

– Harrison Ford,
quote published in Crushable,
"10 Celebrities Who Hate Fame"

Inherent in the wish of fame is the myth that celebrities have it all—however you define 'it'. In a flash, you can become the newest member of what Oprah terms "the fallen celebrity syndrome." Perhaps this is why our voyeuristic society relishes the hard and fast falls from fame's pedestal. Perhaps there is comfort in knowing that no one is above suffering.

To be seen, heard, and acknowledged is a very real and natural human desire. Celebrity meltdowns are largely the result of the right spiritual thirst but the wrong drink, to borrow a phrase from Swiss psychotherapist Carl Jung. Fame is the icing on the cake of life—with little or no nutrition. While it tastes sweet, consuming too much will lead to a host of problems. Even if you perpetually had all of the neon in Las Vegas shining upon you, it wouldn't be enough to brighten a spirit left in the dark. External validation is a strobe: it's bright and fast, but fleeting and leaves you in the dark. One false move and the same set of qualities that were once considered endearing by a fickle public become tiresome. It takes very little time for their adulation and love to transform into anger and hatred. You can only be truly be lit from within.

In a situation where you are constantly surrounded by adulation or attention, it is natural to wish for respite, an island of calm in the midst of the storm. This will inevitably lead you to resort to different means in order to insulate yourself from the onslaught of the public eye. Often, this means reducing your trusted circle to a small entourage or a group of friends. The trouble is that even the people surrounding you are not entirely immune to the trappings of fame its all too common to succumb leading to a state of depersonalization or alienation.

In order to stay unaffected by fame, you unwittingly isolate yourself, and before you realize, it you are alone on an island surrounded by people who you don't even really know. Learn to recognize the signs of emotional agoraphobia before it envelops you and pervades your reasoning, preventing you from differentiating what is real and what is make believe (or delusional). The first thing you need to do is figure out who your real friends are and who are just followers of fame.

Loneliness, Isolation, and Trust

No one really wants to admit they are lonely, and it's never really addressed very much between friends and family. But I have felt lonely many times in my life.

– Bill Murray

People flock to you. Thousands, possibly millions, of fans surround you. You're out-and-about, meeting new people every day as you soar higher and higher in your career. You're beginning to understand the old adage it's lonely at the top. People need to feel as though they belong, to feel part of a community having shared experiences. Your community of peers is small and dispersed. Not many people share your unique experiences.

If you feel all alone or isolated, you're not alone. You in the company of A-list star Jennifer Lawrence, who has publicly admitted that her newfound fame created a lonely lifestyle. While she loves the people she works with and has good personal relationships, her travel schedule isolates her from spending a great deal of time with those who truly know her and who don't care about her star status. Your quality of life rests on your ability to share in the experience and connect with other people successfully. When the people you want to share with most are not around (or elusive), its understandable to feel lost in the maze of public isolation.

George Clooney revealed that it could get lonely even when surrounded by other people because he's often put in isolation. He feels loneliest in public arenas because he'll end up in the smallest compartment possible. His presence is a distraction to everybody. He ends up not being able to enjoy an event like everyone else.

Rihanna thought fame was a dream come true until she realized how often she's left alone without the people she loves. Kim Cattrall's career kept her focus away from building a relationship and starting a family. Now she feels as if she missed out on a "normal life" as she accepts the price she's paid to build her career.

There's a difference between wanting to be alone and wanting to be left alone. When people are with you just to get something, tangible or intangible, for their own benefit, you may rightly want to be left alone. This doesn't mean you want to be by yourself. You want to be around those who are with you because there is a mutual exchange of respect, interests, and friendship. Everything's on the table and there are no hidden agendas in the relationship. It's disheartening when you find yourself surrounded by people you can't trust. The poet, T.S. Eliot wrote, "What loneliness is more lonely than distrust?"

Justin Bieber says he doesn't have many friends because there aren't a lot of people he can trust. He ends up feeling down, gloomy, and lonely when there's no one to talk to. When you can't trust others, you feel like you have to be on constant guard to keep your place or prevent your destruction. When you feel locked-up, constantly watched, see your family space violated, or experience a familiarity that breeds an inappropriate closeness, you lose your grip on a sense of basic safety and security. Extraordinary talent, fame, financial success, and an adoring public is an inadequate deterrent or remedy from the subjective experience of isolation.

It's true that if you don't want information or stories about you available for public consumption then you can't speak of it to anyone. Accept this circumstance as part of the territory of celebrity. This doesn't mean that no one is trustworthy. Trust yourself first and keep your own confidences. Keep your inner circle of loved ones with whom you confide close and small to limit your potential for unwanted exposure.

When you hire people, give the value of their character highest priority when selecting the best candidate for a particular position. The people you work with are no more and no less than the people you work with. Develop and maintain good professional relationships while keeping the conversations focused on the business at hand. If you're spending most of your time away from your family, check in with them by phone or SKYPE as often as you can. Communicating through text or email won't give you the sense of connection a real conversation provides, especially in unreal circumstances.

There's a part of you that knows who and what to trust: your intuition (informed by experience). Your gut is very wise. It's actually located in the area of your solar plexus. The vast network of nerves surrounding the esophagus, stomach, and intestines contain of a level of complexity that it is sometimes called the "second brain," the brain that feels. The brain in your head thinks. What was once cast off as a simple collection of relay ganglia, scientists now recognize it an independent of the brain proper. Having a mind of its own, it is said that this network transmits information known informally as "gut instincts" and gives rise to the full feeling of satisfaction and the emptiness of discontent.

Pay attention to this innate asset. If you reflect upon the times you didn't listen to your gut, you'll realize that it usually ended up creating a less than wanted experience. When you paid attention to what you intuitively knew, you often fared far better. Discern the difference between an intuitive gut feeling and the sense of fear. Intuition is calming; fear is alarming.

Isolation, loneliness and mistrust are all things you may experience. Work through those feelings by enriching the relationship you have with yourself, making choices in alignment with what you value, and trust your own wisdom when it presents itself as your loyal guide.

Get Real About Power

Fame is a delicate and dangerous creature. I saw people who didn't honor it, who refused to take responsibility for it, get destroyed by it. I also saw that stardom in and of itself was empty.
– Patrick Dempsey

Fame, money, and success aren't what give you the power to live a free, powerful, and full life. Your experiences shape how you feel about the quality of your existence and are formed and informed by your inner dialog. What gives you the freedom and power you desire comes from the fortitude and conviction you have to wield three mighty magic wands: responsibility, integrity, and accountability.

I can hear you groan. Those three words sucked the energy right out of you. Some part of you had it mean, and it all sounded like a burden. Don't worry. I'm not going to shove airy-fairy bullshit down your throat to tell you how to manifest your miracles. I'm also not going to be the one to kick your ass if you're like a lot of people who don't know quite what to do with themselves once they become successful.

The simple fact is: no one can do anything for or to you. When it comes to experiencing your highest potential and all the magic that comes with that deliciousness, no one can serve it up to you on a silver platter or the red carpet. Like it or not, it's completely up to you. To get you started, let's shift your perspective a bit so you can get energized (rather than exhausted) when you think of what it means to be responsible and accountable with integrity.

Responsibility starts with the willingness to see yourself as the absolute creator and director of your life. Responsibility, in this context, has nothing to do with judgment. Fault, praise, blame, shame, credit, or guilt has nothing to do with being responsible. I believe everyone does the best they can with the light they have to see. True, some people are wandering around dark alleys with no batteries in their flashlight. While they may bang into wall after wall after wall, they're still doing the best they can with their limited perspective.

Blaming, criticizing, or feeling guilty adds no light to the situation. It only draws the curtains further closed. You can't band-aid your way out of your circumstances. Face the role you played in creating whatever is going on. You can't just cover up the blemish or pretend it isn't there. Figuring out new and different ways to get out of the dark alley will begin to light the path. When you look at your situations from the point of view that you are the source of what you are, what you do, and how you experience your life, you give yourself the inner light to guide you through any alley, no matter how dark.

When you take this stand, you will never be a victim of anyone or anything ever again. You realize life happens *for* you rather than *to* you. When you examine the events of your life, good and bad, from a position of responsibility, you give yourself the opportunity for growth and expansion. Searching to distinguish the role you played in creating your situation and experience of it will give you the information to think and act differently the next time around if you aren't happy with your outcome. You'll also discover the hidden recipe in how you created your good results enabling you to create more of the good stuff in the future.

In ethics, integrity is regarded as the honesty and accuracy of one's actions. Integrity regards consistency of character to be a virtue.

When you function from the foundation of integrity, you act in accordance with the values, beliefs, and principles you claim to hold. In other words, to act with integrity is to walk your talk.

People of integrity hold themselves answerable to their values, beliefs, and principles. Their values systems provide a framework within which they act. Individuals with integrity are aligned with their own best beliefs. But integrity should not be mistaken for perfection. In any area you struggle, you are likely to be "out of alignment" or in some fashion. Your choices and actions that are not in alignment with your core values will feel disconnected instead of whole.

The most concrete example of your integrity in action is your financial situation. When your career takes off, you cross the chasm from barely making it to rolling in it. With financial resources come many more options. Unexpectedly, decisions that were once easy become complicated. When you don't have any money, deciding whether or not to buy something is easier because you can't even if you want to. When you've got bucks, you have to make money decisions you never thought you'd face.

When you make more, it's easy to spend more. When you plug your value system into your decision-making process, best options reveal themselves. If you value education, for example, you'll put money aside for you're children's college fund. Education is more important than a Swarovski-studded iPhone. Integrity encourages you to think about what you want the values your life reflects.

Keep priorities in order. When you do it right, people who know you won't see much difference in what matters most to you in how you live. Knowing that fame is fleeting, consider maintaining practicality with your expenditures while enjoying a little more peace of mind in your new financial status. A million dollars sounds like a lot, but it can be gone in a flash with an overpriced real estate purchase. An apartment building, for example, will pay much more over time than a flashy mansion. Smart money choices will help cement your ability to live comfortably however fleeting (or lasting) your celebrity may be.

The most famous maxim of Socrates is to "Know thyself." Do not boast beyond your truth. Pay no attention to the opinion of the multitude. Stay in alignment with who you really are, what you value, and for which you stand. Such integrity requires honesty. When you follow through with your word and are impeccable and honorable with your actions, you generate respect, confidence in your abilities, and an attitude of professionalism with others. You treat others as you would like to be treated. Time commitments and investments are honored rather than wasted. Confidences are kept. Your word is your promise and contract. You have of respect for yourself and for others, and they hold you in high regard. A life rooted in integrity is freer, without unnecessary encumbrances and drama.

A principled attitude doesn't stop when you reach success. There is great temptation to think only in terms of what you can sell or what is expected upon you once you've received recognition for your work. When you think only of what will put more money in the bank instead of what inspires you, that inner burning that wants to be expressed starts to die out. For example, if you're a writer, you may default to writing what you believe will be a serviceable script. It won't have a unique voice. It will be a submission that could have been delivered by any number of other writers. By placing yourself in such a pigeonhole, you never let your specialness fully develop. You'll feel the discontentment that comes with sequestering your unique expression. Never put your inspiration aside for very long if you want to rise above mediocrity. Don't be afraid to be special and singular and know that being unique is not a virtue when it is impenetrable or simply bad.

Aristotle knew a thing or two about making a positive emotional connection with those to whom you communicate. Know your audience. If you want people to hear and value what you have to say, you have to understand—and communicate that awareness—of their beliefs, attitudes, age, education level, language, and culture. The more you know about the audience of your message and brand, the better able you will be to tell your story in a way that will be heard, understood, and appreciated.

Accountability is the third piece of the power pie. You need to hold yourself accountable to what you say you want to achieve. Being responsible and a person of integrity takes courage, conviction, and commitment. It's easy to obligate yourself when there's no stress. When you're facing the demands and expectations of your profession, the tendency to justify or make excuses for deviation or abandonment can be overwhelming. The truth is, you can't do everything for everyone, and that means making choices that are true to you, true to the nature of your work, and true to fulfilling your needs (which may or may not coincide with your desires).

Identify three to five of your primary professional and personal goals. Share them with someone who knows you well, someone who can track your progress and call you on your babblecrap when you serve up reasons for defaulting on your obligations to yourself. Keep your objectives at the top of your mind each and every day.

Imagine who would you need to be, what would you need to do and have, in order to succeed in accomplishing your achievement. Ask yourself: am I behaving, choosing, and acting in a way that is consistent that vision? If you slip, notice the setback without judgment. Any moment you spend beating yourself, or anyone else, up is a wasted moment. Just look at the situation from the position of responsibility, make the course correction, and step forward again in that direction.

Before we close on the three elements of power, it's important to make the distinction between the word "power" and the word "force." As we are discussing it here, *power* is generated from the strength of will, an action generated from within; *force* is an attempt to get someone to do something against his or her will, by manipulating or coercing someone to bend to your will. Power influences where force demands. Power is generated through positive direction while force is fueled by negative intentions. You were born to be the source of power in all that you create.

Keep Private Matters Private

I don't like to share my personal life. It wouldn't be personal if I shared it.

– George Clooney

The issue of privacy produces another paradox. Wanting a quiet retreat isn't the same thing as coveting secrecy. Celebrity alters your way of life, affecting the interpersonal space in which you live, play, and work. The important "personal" boundary is often breeched. Every move must be considered. It isn't easy to straddle to work within, yet live outside, the entertainment industrial complex. If you want others to value your privacy, you have to value it yourself. This means you must be vigilant about keeping your private life private.

Want to lie out by your backyard pool wearing your favorite itsy bitsy teeny-weeny bikini? Forget about it—if you don't want your cellulite to be featured on grocery store tabloids. Go to a remote location to do your nearly nude sunbathing. Want to take your toddler to the park? Think again—if you don't want your child to be frightened by the hoards of cameras vying to capture her cute little smile. Go to another high-profile friend's who has a young child and let them play together on the walled lawn? Go through a painful break-up? Expect to find the details reported throughout the Twittersphere. You may even be surprised to find out you're already in a new relationship with someone you've never met according to the aisles in the supermarket (which you can no longer stand in). Know that you're a juicy target for hackers. Don't keep anything on your computer or cell phone you don't want to see in the tabloids. Never do anything you wouldn't want to explain to the paramedics. Your life is now on TV, it's own reality show.

While you desire and deserve the rights of any other private individual, you also embody a public brand. The First Amendment protects free speech. It doesn't protect each and every instance of privacy invasion. In fact, it defers to "freedom of the press," so unless an article is specifically defaming you through lies, the press can print nearly anything they way. Also, be aware that different rules of privacy are applied internationally. What is invasion of privacy in LA may well be good journalism in London.

Keeping your children and other family members out of the media can be a challenge. Family, especially children, of stars haven't chosen fame. They're thrown into the limelight just because they're related to you. The public is fascinated by the new generation of stars growing up, so information about and pictures of those you love the most are in demand. To have some stranger follow, photograph, and confront your child is terrifying.

In the landmark J.K. Rowling case in Great Britain the courts ruled that children of celebrities have the same privacy rights as all children with regard to privacy. In France, it's illegal to photograph a child without permission. At least in the United States, your right to privacy is more vigorously upheld in the courts.

Testifying at a hearing, rock legends Mick Fleetwood and Steven Tyler convinced a Hawaii Senate committee in early 2013 to approve a bill, the so-called "Steven Tyler Act," to protect celebrities and anyone else from intrusive paparazzi. Tyler asked Sen. Kalani English to introduce the legislation after the paparazzi captured an image of Tyler and his girlfriend in his home, publishing it as part of a story reporting the two were about to be wed. The issue, for Tyler, wasn't as much about the photo as it was about what it revealed. Tyler hadn't confided the engagement to his family. The bill gives people the power to sue others who take photos or video of their private lives in an offensive way, such as using a telephoto lens or other advanced equipment to record them on their private properties. However, such bans are often limited by geographic location (such as by state) and can vary widely. Live your new life cautiously.

Enacting more laws isn't the decisive answer. Besides, how do you legislate good behavior? Until the masses take a stand and a society and stops buying magazines that feature their favorite stars—something that's not likely to happen in our lifetime—it is up to you to mindfully manage and monitor your exposure and the exhibition of your family.

When I ask clients (and most anyone else I know) what fame and fortune will give them, the answer is always freedom to do anything and everything whenever and wherever. Yet the reality is often quite the opposite. Public opinion holds that celebrities deserve, and should expect, to have their privacy rights revoked. Angelina Jolie, Jennifer Aniston, and Jennifer Lopez live much of their life trapped like a bird in a gilded cage. There are many who feel imprisoned by their persona.

Today, the ubiquitous and viral culture of the Internet the public becomes judge and jury for the notorious and those who were just caught up under fame's wing unwittingly. Inherent in freedom is the ability to shape and direct your reputation. Popular iconic stars such as Elvis, Michael Jackson, and Marilyn Monroe are just a few cautionary tales of those who suffered greatly from the relentless public scrutiny. For the professional and public paparazzi, everything is fair game when it comes to capturing your most private moments and personal secrets. The more personal and the more private, the better. Your personal life can easily become a story for the masses to define you through the media lens. When it comes to privacy, imagine yourself as an onion. Decide how many layers you're going to peel off and expose to the public.

Paparazzi Perils

*Celebrity and secrets don't go together. The bastards
will get you in the end.*
                                    – *George Michael*

At first, it's wonderful to be photographed in recognition for your work. If you continue to shine, the game is on. You'll be hunted, pursued, like prey. Instead of celebrating who you are and what you've done, the media is on a quest to uncover the "real person" behind the public persona. An extremely exciting day for a reporter or blogger is when he finds something—or lots of somethings—wrong with you, or finding something they can spin that way. What sells magazines and attracts eyeballs to other media content are stories and images of idolized people at their lowest.

Chief among the badgers are the paparazzi. The term paparazzi is defined as a freelance photographer, especially one who takes candid pictures of celebrities for publication. The connotation of the term is much stronger that just freelance cameramen who shoot stars. The paparazzi are often viewed as annoying persistent photographers who stalk their celebrity victims and go to any length to get the shot they want.

You've been there, faced with a sea of cameras in your face. It's very disorienting. You can't see in front of you. Imprisoned by the herd, you can't move or get to where you want to go. You feel like a caged rat or treated like an object—as if you weren't human. Since everyone has a camera now, anyone has the potential to sell a piece of you. You feel completely exposed. Those with prominence go to great lengths to avert a public appearance. Mark Anthony and Jennifer

83

Lopez, while dating, hid in the trunk of a friend's car to travel from one place to another to hide from the media hordes.

How do you deal with the perils of the paparazzi? You can beat your chest about it, analyze the who, what, why and how to death about it—or chose to accept it and decide how you want to live. Start by staying poised. Keep calm. Carry on. Maintain (as much as possible) a studied awareness of your body, feelings, and mind. Seriously consider every word you utter. Monitor anxiety and anger, because they will certainly unravel everything you've worked so hard to put together. If you're down deep in the media chasm of a misguided situation, remember the first rule of holes: if you're in one, stop digging.

There are ways to turn a hellish experience into an opportunity. Celebrity couple Andrew Garfield and Emma Stone used the paparazzi attention to spread some goodness. When the photographers caught them outside a restaurant, they used the moment to bring attention to an organization they care about, Worldwide Orphan's Foundation and Gilda's Club NYC. They quickly penned and held-up signs for the cameras that said, "We just found out that there are paparazzi outside the restaurant we were eating in. So…why not take this opportunity to bring attention to organizations that need and deserve it? www.wwo. org, www.GildasClubNYC.org. Have a great day!" Use the paparazzi. Why not? They're using you.

The stars and the masses often criticize the methods used by the paparazzi as an invasion of the privacy rights of celebrities. It get's a bit tricky because a lot of what the camera captures occurs in public places where the right to privacy is greatly limited. Over the years, the right of privacy has developed to protect against four main types of invasions: (1) intrusion into solitude, (2) public disclosure of private facts, (3) depiction in a false light, and (4) commercial exploitation of a person's name or likeness, also known as appropriation. These rights apply to private and public figures, at least in theory. The sad truth is, you will have a much harder time recovering for an invasion of privacy than a private individual. The paparazzi can use newsgathering and newsworthiness defenses to protect their actions. The press has a right to inform the public about matters of public interest, and as a high-profile personality, the public is very much interested in you and how you live your life. What constitutes news and entertainment becomes more and more comingled with every passing day.

What makes being a public person trying to have some semblance of a private life even more arduous is when the media gets in your face *because* photographers and reporters want to rile you. They want to provoke and capture a reaction from you. And the image likely won't be in your favor. While a photograph is accurate (assuming Photoshop wasn't used), it doesn't express the truth. A photograph tells the story of one tiny slice, just in a moment of time. What it doesn't offer is context. It's common to see reaction shots placed next to unrelated stories to offer a biased editorial point of view. Also, many photographs are presented purely from the perspective of the photographer who views situations through his personal lens, figuratively and literally.

A paparazzo's goal is to heighten your reaction because the most outrageous shots or retorts get the most money. Getting the "money shot" has become an aggressive, competitive sport. The rivalry for your attention is so fierce that some will team up to snare you in their trap. One will confront you so the other one can photograph or record the ordeal. The sharpest of shooters have a network of informants to report on your whereabouts. They'll get the shot they want no matter what—even if they have to break the law. The potential reward is too great to miss. Forget about trying to reason with disrespectful members of the media. Your pleas for consideration will fall on deaf ears.

Why invite trouble for yourself by giving the media by giving them the prize? If you want to pay their mortgage, cut the photographers and abrasive interviewers a check. It's a lot easier than risking your reputation with an out-of-context rejoinder. Why let yourself become labeled as the jerk, bully, victim, ice queen, or maniac? While the paparazzi may keep you in the news, they don't keep your career alive—at least not for very long.

Never, ever attack as a means of defense. States have laws against aggravated assault. This means no punching, grabbing, kicking, or smashing a photographer's camera. If the cops are called, you'll find a very different photo of you in the morning's newspaper: your mug shot. And it won't be pretty. So, watch your temper. Manage your triggers. Keep calm. Carry on.

To bypass adverse press, be boring in public. To keep your image engaging instead of tiresome, reinvent yourself in a genuine way from time to time. Keep your audience interested and captivated by doing and being good, positive, and generous. Develop a choreographed strategy that enriches your character rather than diminishes. Since the media and the masses are hungry for candid shots of you and yours, shoot and submit them yourself through a third party. I'm not kidding. Have a friend take a photo of your at the grocery store, restaurant, or walking down the street. Any regular setting will do. The better the quality of the image the more likely it will be chosen over similar yet poorer quality images. It's worth a shot (if you can forgive the pun). Also think carefully about where you live. Many of the high profile that can choose to live anywhere other than Los Angeles, considered Ground Zero for the Paparazzi. If you must live in LA-LA land, keep an eye out for real estate listings featuring gated security to *stopperrazzi*.

Without the media and an eager public that devours celebrity gossip, the paparazzi wouldn't exist. They wouldn't be able to earn a living. The irony is that much of the public has little regard for the paparazzi—yet they can't get enough of their work product.

While you may have trouble maintaining a cause of action against paparazzi invasions, the media hounds are not completely licensed to do as they wish to gather information. Trespass laws do exist to protect you while you are on private property. Even so, that won't stop a helicopter hovering over your house, enabling a photographer armed with a powerful zoom lens from trying to capture a shot of you or your family if you're outside of Hawaii. A determined photographer with proper monetary motivation will get the shot, so always live as if you're being observed.

Each state has its own laws regarding privacy. New York and California provide the most extensive regulations for protecting privacy interests, probably due to the relatively high concentration of public figures in these two states. Check the laws in your state to get a better understanding of what you're up against. When you travel internationally, check the laws in each country if you are concerned about your privacy. It's okay to let your lawyer or assistant do the actual research, but make sure it gets done and make sure they summarize it accurately so you understand it.

Romance and Rendezvous

Money and success don't change people; they merely amplify what's already there.

– Will Smith

In a world where so many people want to shine under your reflection, your opportunities for relationships of all kinds are unprecedented. Dale Launer weighed in on this issue based on his own and the experiences of close personal friends. Launer knows how it feels to go from having beautiful women never give you a second look to having these same women readily offer themselves up for booty calls. While flattering, it's hard to develop or sustain an honest intimate relationship with someone who would still stick with you even if you landed in movie jail. He became rather disgusted with himself when he kept coming up with outlandish reasons why he had to kick a woman out of his bed and house once the deed was consummated. Resolved to seek quality over quantity, he's now more satisfied in his lovely liaisons.

Men chase women like lions chase antelopes. When the catch is so easy, the risk is coming down with a sad case of what I've heard termed within the community as (politically incorrect) TMP, too much pussy. This dis-ease has befallen celebrities such as Tiger Woods, Russell Brand, Eliot Spitzer, David Duchovny, Jesse James, Kanye West, and Tom Sizemore. Deep and long-term relationships are thwarted in exchange for a series of shallow quickies. The phenomenon isn't limited to men. Women who develop an addiction to sex use it largely as a misguided means to fill an emotional need, perhaps to build their self-esteem through a relationship with the esteemed, rather than achieve a masculine conquest. Either way, left unchecked, too much is ruinous. Lots of people get hurt.

If you are hopping from bed to bed, be responsible. Booty-call beauties can secure their financial future just by having your baby. Don't trust birth control claims. Wear your umbrella. Take your pill if you don't want to have your partner-of-the-moment have a reason to stay connected to you the rest of your life. Remember that when a ridiculous amount of more is better, it's not about sex. It's about obsession.

Close working relationships—where you spend hours, days, weeks, and months collaborating together—create a dangerous self-fulfilling prophecy where marriage and fame don't mix. It happens all the time. Working away from home can cause problems at home. You begin to disconnect because you start to see home as monotonous. A colleague becomes a confidant at work. The convenience of that relationship drives a bigger wedge in the marriage. More confidences are shared that lead to an affair. The affair kills the marriage.

Developing meaningful relationships requires open and honest communication. Are you charming when the subject is about you and bored when the focus is turned to your partner's interests? If so, your relationship will fade as quickly as your span of attention. Continually talking about yourself isn't sharing.

When you want to communicate something that is "true" for you, do so without making someone else wrong for their differing beliefs. Studies have shown that when you want to get a message across, only 7% of what is being processed are your words. Your body language is valued at 55% of the communication and your tone of voice 38%.

Think about it: how often has an email of yours been misunderstood? Whoever "got it wrong" read it through the tone of his or her lens of the world and your relationship at the time. They filled in unwritten meanings into your words through their own "filters."

Delivering a statement is only one half of communication. It has to be heard and understood in the way you intended complete the transaction. You have to say what you mean in a way that can be heard and understood. Shouted words are often not heard and usually misunderstood. Think of the times you've been yelled at. You tend to deflect the words as your arm yourself to fight back or you've fled. Active listening for comprehension was not on your agenda. If you want to be heard and understood, don't yell. Usually the person who is doing the screaming is doing so in a misguided attempt to be heard. Just being with someone and listening, with an open mind and an open heart, can make all the difference in the world when someone is upset or looking for support.

Talk straight. By that I mean tell the truth, have empathy for others, and be complete in your communications. Keep your promises or make amends when it becomes impossible to meet that expectation. If you want to have an honest relationship grounded in respect and trust, you have to show up to that relationship each and every day from a place of honesty, respect, and trust.

A discussion on relationships cannot be complete without addressing love. Most people say they want a loving relationship. What is really wanted is love that is unconditional, something much easier said than done. The fact that most people tend not to love themselves unconditionally makes it difficult to love others without condition. If you were to look at your life today, do you see any relationships where the love you give has expectations attached? Do you see people with whom your love could expand? Where can you be more compassionate, acknowledging, generous, and accepting?

Of course, there are times when you are unwilling to give your love freely, perhaps because you feel as if you've been treated wrongly or that someone hasn't acted lovingly towards you. It's important to see that people live their lives inside of the highest expression of love that is available to them at the time. What this means is that if you want to experience more love, you have to generate it. Sounds a bit weird, I know. But it works.

As an everyday example, if you're annoyed because fans bother you while you're trying to get a bit of shopping done, instead of being annoyed, shift that energy into an appreciation of the fact that they are interested in you. Say a kind word or two before you gracefully excuse yourself. Giving someone an abrupt brush off isn't an act of love. Even if the intruder was a bit rude, you can choose not to respond in kind. One of the reasons people flock to you is because you are recognizable. Deep down inside, many of those who approach you want to be recognized. A positive acknowledgement from you will help them feel seen, heard, and validated. It's a simple thing to do that can have a lasting positive impact.

The most important relationship you'll ever have is the relationship you have with yourself. Take inventory of all the attributes you want in a loving relationship and be that person for yourself. At the very, least you'll really enjoy the time you spend with you.

Winning the Fame Game

Chapter Three
Keeping It Real

I believe there's an inner power that makes winners or losers. And the winners are the ones who really listen to the truth of their hearts.

– Sylvester Stallone

Fame means millions of people have the wrong idea of who you are.

–Erica Jong

1

I am standing alone on the balcony of my hotel room on the fifth floor. It feels almost like a vacation. But it's not. I'm definitely not on vacation. The one I have been long waiting for. Still it almost feels like one. I am here to meet the press for a publicity event arranged for by my agent, later in the day. I see a movement from the corner of my eye and look down. The next thing I know, I am seeing a blur and hearing a roar. There's a crowd below, cameras and noise, eyes and applause. Or is it envy and derision?

2

I sipped my coffee and try to stay awake. I had it on good authority that Joanna Symmonds was staying at the Hotel Excelsior. I thought it was my good fortune that I could get a press badge through my journalist friend so that I could join the hordes of paparazzi awaiting a glimpse of the star. I think I might have dozed off for a moment and was woken up by the noise. I looked at the cameras that were floating above a sea of raised hands and looked up. There she was, up there, a speck, a glimpse, the reward for my sleepless night and more than two hours of early morning vigilance.

The previous page illustrates two points of view: one coming from a celebrity, another from an admirer. You're seen. Who is really recognized? This is one of the many paradoxes of fame.

In the unlikely coincidence that your name is Joanna Symmonds, you know that the above-mentioned person is not you. Though it's about a real celebrity, the real name has been changed. But if you're famous, then it doesn't matter if your name isn't Joanna. It's still about you, in many ways.

Wearing the mask of your media-adorned persona, it's easy to forget you are first and foremost a person who loves and is loved, who can hurt and be hurt. You're not made of pixels. Your happiness isn't defined by the number of likes you have on your Facebook page or your total Twitter followers. You have your strengths and private vulnerabilities. You have dreams and despair.

To be famous is to have a public persona. And that can be a lot of fun. In order to be fulfilled as a human being with fame, you have to have the confidence to be inwardly rooted in your authenticity even while being perceived as that public image. You have to know how to keep it real.

Living the fantasy of a persona full time isn't healthy. It's essential to center your persona in the truth of who you are. This is the distinction I make between "selfish" and "centered." A selfish person is oriented exclusively in his or her own beliefs and needs and lacks consideration for others. A centered person is a person who is aware of the "self," knows his or her truth while including the right of others to be centered in theirs. Being able to be comfortable in your publicly owned character is about having the courage to hold a deeper meaning for what you're really all about while in it.

The truth is that people, including you and me, tend to make assumptions about other people with little or no supporting evidence. We interpret physical and verbal expressions through our own lens of the world and project that view on what we see. Do you look at the picture on a magazine cover and ask yourself, "Uh-oh, is she thinking what I think she's thinking? I can see it in her eyes that she'd rather be somewhere else than facing the camera. Or is it just my imagination?" We rarely look below the surface because it's much easier to make a snap judgment than to peel away the layers of what is behind the neat and tidy packages we see around us.

Take, for instance, the car you drive. It's great from the outside. What do you see? You admire its sleek lines, shiny paint and metal on the exterior, and the wood, leather or fabric on the inside. You know you have grease and oil, gears and pistons grinding and turning away beneath all this, but you aren't interested. These are the not-so-pleasant parts of life that you'd rather not concern yourself with (unless you're into that kind of thing).

What about the coffee you are drinking? Is it a latte in a corrugated paper container with an attractive design of the coffee brand? Or is it in a pristine white ceramic mug with an appetizing aroma wafting from the brown liquid? Do you think of coffee beans roasted and ground? Perhaps yes, if you're drinking your coffee in a café and happen to see a poster on the wall showing oversized coffee beans being scooped up. Why do real coffee beans look so unassuming when compared to their pictures?

That's because things are not really what they appear to be. We see what we've been conditioned to see, mostly by advertising. The average person sees 2,500 ads every day in one shape or another. We're trained by the filter of the media to interpret things a certain way. The public will interpret its vision of you based upon what they've blindly accepted through headline journalism or through other third party sources. Being seen as someone you aren't can be upsetting. Buying into other's adoption of that image will only further disconnect you from who you really are, causing you even more despair. The only remedy is to not inhibit yourself by pretending to be something you're not or giving your persona more value than your true nature. It's not easy, I know. We all want to be seen, heard, and acknowledged for who we really are. And you have little or no control over what others may think of you. This means you have to see, hear, and acknowledge yourself. It also helps to spend a lot of time around others who do know the person behind your persona.

Maintain a perspective on what really matters to you. Never trade in integrity for temporary gain. Maintain your credibility by staying true to your commitments. Remember where you came from as you evolve over time. Don't lie or alter yourself in any significant way merely to appeal to someone else.

Most importantly: be in and stay in touch with the person you were born to become. Who are you? What do you do? Are the answers to these two questions the same?

Isn't who you're defined by what you do? Someone is a singer because that's what he or she does. Someone else is an automobile mechanic because that's what he does. That girl over there in the café is a barista because she makes and serves you your coffee. That face on the cover of the magazine belongs to an industrial titan, an actress, a writer, or the leader of a nation.

Is your mother a dentist or a lawyer? No, she is neither. She's a woman: a human being with feelings, desires, fears, hopes, dreams and perspective. She also happens to be your mother.

People are not what they do. They are who they are. Who you are and what you do are two different things. To stay rooted in your reality, you have to develop and maintain three healthy attitudes: an appreciation for a positive relationship with your self, maintain a healthy relationship with money and success, and keep a reasonable perspective of your place in the world. The circumstance of your life is never the issue. How you relate to the circumstances of your life is the issue. How you relate to yourself as you go through your life is also the issue.

Keeping it real is also about staying present. Many people spend most of their lives stuck in the past or dreaming (or worrying) about the future. The trouble with that is no time is spent in the here and now, where life happens. Henry David Thoreau famously said: "Life is what happens to you when you're making other plans." It's the only moment you have when you can be the driver instead of the effect of your life. Nothing really exists outside this present moment, this very second. Oops, that one's gone. There goes another one.

The past and the future are illusions based on our interpretations of them, not necessarily on reality. Reality is infinitely complex. You can only deal with the here and now, with your limited scope of influence in the present moment. When your head is in the past, you tend to create more incidents that resemble the past. When your head is in the future, you also tend to make decisions that repeat your past because they are informed by the same thinking that resulted in those experiences. You have to be present, awake, and aware to make a deliberate change in thinking through lessons learned. That's how unwanted patterns of behavior are transformed into ones that produce desired outcomes.

The times you've spent fully in the present are the moments you felt "in the zone." You were energized, focused, and firing on all cylinders. You were unaware of the passage of time, and you felt good.

The stress from demands and obligations will inevitably yank you out of your Zen-zone-ness. That's OK. Just be aware of when it happens. You can still stay mostly present by being attentive, as a non-judgmental observer, to your thoughts and feelings as they come and go. Challenge the ones that consume all your energy. Ride the ones that motivate and inspire. If you're running a sob story in your head or in your conversations, change it up. Give it a new ending by telling it through a different perspective. Purposefully and naturally enrich the quality of your experience right now. And now.

Powerful Persona Formula

To me, the main thing about living on this planet is to know who you are and be real about it. That's the reason I'm still alive.

– Keith Richards

What I am going to reveal here is a potent formula to stay on course during your journey as a celebrity. It is a simple enough equation, but it will enable you to navigate the labyrinth that you will certainly encounter when your wagon is hooked to wild dragon we call Fame.

The formula is: **Presence * Purpose = Powerful Persona** (P*P=P2)

Your **Powerful Persona** (your brand image) = **Presence** (how you show up in the world which includes being 'present' in the moment, always) * **Purpose** (passionate conviction for what you wish to create or achieve).

To have a powerful persona, exude an enduring magnetic personality. You will attract others by how good you make them feel in your presence. Just being with you will give them a sense of validation and empowerment. When you show up in a state of genuine self-confidence, people are naturally drawn to you.

Those who are powerless as a persona have difficulty connecting with others. They may be thought of as brilliant but not well liked. They may be too stiff, always look nervous, or behave too strongly or be too intense. Those with a personality in opposition or conflict with itself may show a lack of confidence, ramble, or be high strung. In their way of being, they repel instead of attract. It's an exhausting way to live.

To develop a Powerful Persona, you first have to know who you really are. You are aligned with who you really are if you like and feel comfortable in the "skin you're in." If you wish you were someone else or uncomfortable with who you are being, chances are you have taken on a personality that you think will help you deal with day-to-day pressures rather than allow yourself to just "be." When I speak of knowing who you are, I'm not talking about your title, occupation, or claim to fame. Who you are is much bigger. Who are you at the core of your soul? What rocks your world? What angers you? For what are you willing to take a stand? What are your vulnerabilities? What are your deepest desires? What keeps you up at night? What gives you courage? Who do you love? What do you value most? The sum of your responses will paint a portrait of your true essence. Get grounded in that profile.

A quote attributed to both Irish novelist C. S. Lewis and Scottish author George MacDonald eloquently invites you consider that you are not even your body. You are not flesh and blood.

You don't have a soul.

You are a Soul.

You have a body.

The public figure that you think you have become (thanks to your fame) is not the *real* you. It is definitely a part of your personality, but it is not entirely who you are. It is important to make this distinction. Otherwise, you could become a commodity that people would like to peer at and examine just like you would a car in a showroom or a purse on a shelf.

Your persona, or brand image, will be crafted from bits and pieces of your true essence, beginning with your values. Your values represent your beliefs, what you cherish, what guides your decisions, and what shapes how you think—and therefore act. Values that resonate with you bring you happiness and joy when present in your life. You get sad and disconnected when they're missing.

Even if it crossed your mind, I can guarantee you money isn't what you value. Ben Franklin once said, "He that is of the opinion money will do everything may well be suspected of doing everything for money." If you think that if you earn a set sum of money you will be happy, it isn't the money you're after. What you're after is the happiness, respect, acknowledgment, enviable lifestyle, or whatever that amount of money will give you. The trouble is, money can deliver none of those things. That's why that number is fleeting: once reached it becomes "not enough" and a new number takes its place. Happiness, respect, acknowledgment, and the sense of self-worth that you hope will come with a rich and famous lifestyle cannot be bought. They can only come from within. If you can't be happy with who you are now you will have difficulty being happy with who you are when you reach your "number." Wherever you go and with whatever you have, there you are.

Make a list of your primary values. When you dig deep, reveal your *real* values, not what you think you *should* value. For example, many people consider family as one of their highest values. If you come from a family-from-hell or have no desire to create one, let go of any compulsion to list family as something you most value. Be honest with yourself, especially if you value honesty. Once you've identified your top values, integrate them into your public persona. If you don't, you're sure to derail at some point because you'll fight against yourself.

From this firm foundation of principles, continue to develop your public persona as you would a character you might play or script. When in public, show up playing that role. Remember, if you're rooted in your authenticity, your persona is genuinely sourced. Stepping into your persona will feel natural.

Empower your presence. When you show up are you confident? Are you tuned-in or checked-out? Do you live in your head or in the moment? Are you actively listening to what someone is saying or just waiting your turn to talk? Do you act and communicate with purpose or do you just wing it directionless? There's a difference between relying on spontaneous intuition, grounded in your innate wisdom, and randomly winging it. The former is soul guided, the latter is often directed by fear and insecurity. You'll know the difference by your results. Guidance of your soul will create magical outcomes. Perfunctory reactions will get in your way, every time.

How would people who know you describe your character? Do you convey integrity and good will? Are you sincere? Do you naturally inspire excellence in those you influence? Do you look for and find the gift, the silver lining, in every experience. Sometimes it takes a sense of humor to be able to shine light upon a dark situation. Are you able to think clearly even under pressure? Do you accept responsibility? Are you self-disciplined?

Can you articulate the humility of your heart? If you can you have the magic to profoundly connect with anyone you meet. A voice that speaks from the heart touches the heart.

Your Purpose is your reason for doing what you do each and every day. What drives you? What is your mission? What do you want to accomplish, *really*? Is it to win an Academy Award? If so, make choices every day that support that goal. Even if you're a proven actor, director, or rock star, spewing your prejudices violently, publicly, and frequently won't win you any favors among the award voting elite. As if plagued by a deadly disease, you'll be left stranded without acknowledgement even for a killer performance.

As a brand, you're bought because you serve an appealing purpose. As a persona, how you perform on stage speaks to your talent and your choices. How you behave offstage is intricately linked to the appeal that your brand personality develops to contribute to the business of being famous. Stay on purpose, and posterity will then preserve it.

Bring your purpose into the present moment. In order to reach your goal in the future, you have to feel and express the energy of its accomplishment now. Using the same Academy Award example, if you were to win the award in two years, what would you be doing today? Who would you be meeting? What would you be learning or perfecting? How would you be feeling and behaving? Being on purpose requires a focused commitment and a harmonic integration of mind, body, and soul.

Acknowledge and embrace your real self—all of it. Every bit of you has meaning and purpose divinely provided to give you what you need to use and to teach you what you need to know. If you get caught up in the frenzy of the flashing lights, you'll be blinded to the guidance you already have within you. Instead of tapping into your personal GPS, you'll succumb, the hapless victim of the onslaught of constant attention. You'll follow the path of from which few return.

Compartmentalize

The image is one thing and the human being is another. It's very hard to live up to an image...put it that way.

– Elvis Presley

Despite what marketers and advertising professionals will tell you, the package is not the person. The package may not be dispensable, but it is disposable. The person is not.

You may have created a personal brand with your inimitable style. Recognize it for what it is, part-and-parcel of the celebration of fame. When the party is over, will you be able to still enjoy your life? Will you still have those whom you can trust and who care for you? Or will you be all alone because you wandered so far way, engulfed so completely in the flame of fame that you are no longer a person?

There are healthy and unhealthy ways to separate different aspects of your life into categories or compartments. The healthy approach is to use it to deal with the reality of your complicated life without going bonkers. A good example is how a person can react calmly in a critical emergency, putting aside fear and pain to focus fully on bringing the situation to a satisfactory resolution. Unhealthy compartmentalization occurs when unconsciously implemented as a defense mechanism to rationalize conflicting values, cognitions, beliefs, etc. within one's self. Selling your character, boxing up guilt, or justifying an atrocious deed will eventually debilitate you. Without going into it any further, I'll leave the discussion on detrimental compartmentalization to the psychologists. *You* can positively use compartmentalization to consciously prioritize and manage the dual nature of your life as a public branded personality and as a private authentic individual.

Keep your private and public life apart. Separate the person from the packaged persona. Maintaining a private profile doesn't mean hiding your lifestyle. Inherent in hiding is an aspect of insecurity or shame regarding one's actions or choices. An overt choice to withhold certain information and exposure is necessary to your personal security.

Remember that the package cannot exist without the person, but the person can exist without the package, especially when prepared and empowered. Keep the people you love and those who love the real person that is you separate from those who love the package. Those who love you will be there always, but you cannot expect those who love the public package to stay with you when there is no reason to do so.

If you don't want to see the details of your private life in the news don't make them newsworthy. It isn't your job to satisfy public curiosity. It is insatiable and will feed off of the innermost aspects of your life if you let it.

In a conversation with Angie Bowie (actress, musician and the former wife of musician David Bowie), she said that it is with great glee we're seeing more of a turn towards people starting to understand that the accumulation of wealth and fame without happiness and without some sort of personal satisfaction, of providing a service of some sort in whatever your game is as an artist, is empty. For Angie, fame and all that came with it was a job not a lifestyle, and it was only a small part of her identity.

The necessity to compartmentalize was also strongly advocated by Ben Watkins, friend and quadruple threat—actor, writer, producer, and director. He's seen a lot of people in the industry become disenchanted because they equate success as an actor (writer, director, etc.) with whether or not they've booked a job. When you decide to become an actor, you don't make a decision to book jobs. You choose to act and create compelling characters. Booking a paying acting job only serves as a validation of that decision—if you need external evidence of the rightness of your choice. Actors pursue acting without regard to compensation.

Generating revenue to provide for your family is in a different compartment. You can satisfy your desire to act and find other ways to provide for your family. Similarly, you can meet the needs of your family without getting an acting job. There are other ways to generate income. Watkins is an actor who has a beautiful wife and three young children. To support his family in between acting opportunities, he developed other marketable skills as a director and staff writer. As an actor, Watkins was always at the mercy of someone else creating something for him. As a writer, he could create his own content. Even if his script didn't sell, it could get him a job. And it did. His success as a seven-season writer for the USA Network show *Burn Notice* led to his advancement to Executive Producer in addition to his writing credits. And he got a chance to play a substantial role in a couple of episodes. Branching out gives Watkins a variety of avenues in which to get the bills paid while his love of acting remains fresh and exciting.

Be methodical about the business side of acting with the understanding that it has nothing to do with your talent or ability. If you tie your ability to provide for your family to your success in landing lucrative roles then you set yourself up for bitterness to seep in. You may find yourself resenting your family or giving up your dream.

Handling Toxic (and Tedious) Trash Talk

I don't think I realized that the cost of fame is that it's open season on every moment of your life.
– Julia Roberts

The topic of celebrity and its subjects is now infotainment that focuses on the minutia of how stars live their lives. Our modern culture perversely seems to take pleasure in the pain of others. Trash-talk infests our culture like an infectious disease. The plethora of disparaging remarks about individual celebrities is legion. Celebrity bashing has become a common pastime in our society.

Aviva Drescher remembers a time when she was shocked and appalled by the amount of hate and venom in the comments she read about her admission on *Real Housewives of New York* that she was afraid to fly. Her husband caught her compulsion to check and view comments and told her to stop reading that crap. Drescher began to lose faith in humanity for the mean-spirited name-calling and mocking directed at her through social media. Drescher thought her revelations about her fear of flying would show her humanity. Instead, she was harshly criticized and made fun of for obsessing over an anxiety, a weakness.

There were some heart-felt positive reactions, especially for the episode where she, through her philanthropic activities, gave prosthetic legs to a child who was an amputee. Drescher lost her left foot in an accident when she was six years old. To mitigate the pain and suffering, she elected to have revisional amputation to remove the leg from the knee down. Even as a child, she has always been driven to never let the accident define her.

It's a shock to be faced with the hateful, malignant comments of the nameless and faceless. You will be criticized for the way you dress, what you say (or didn't say), what you feed your kids, the breed of dog you adopted, what you eat, who you hang out with, where you live, and just about every other choice you make. It's one thing to be open to criticism. Being subjected to cruelty day-in/day-out requires a strong resilience.

When you walk across a floor that's squeaky clean, you know that it has just been mopped and cleaned. You can almost smell the disinfectant trying to gloss over the faint residue emanating from whatever obnoxious and ungainly stuff was spilled just a moment ago. There is no evidence to prove that something unpleasant happened because the floor is squeaky clean, but there is a lurking suspicion that something is amiss. When celebrities live an all too public private life that is picture perfect, the media and the audience naturally expects to see a glimpse of the ugly beneath the beautiful, the dirty beneath the clean, the chaos beneath the order. It's natural to expect that a squeaky clean life hides many a sordid secret. No matter how careful you are, the media will find something to put a spot on you, to make you look messy. When that happens, the revenue generating business you carefully built on your fame crumbles because your celebrity appeal is what keeps the wheels in motion. In the midst of a runaway media assault, the number of your Twitter followers may skyrocket but your reputation and bankability will be diminished.

Naysayers exist to pounce upon even the tiniest hint of disgrace. Rumors of the details of your marriage, divorce, tip-offs on improper liaisons, scandals, and sexual indiscretions are daily bread for the press. They feed upon your discretions like wasps on caterpillars, stinging you at every chance.

It's odd how people are more ready to line up in the criticism than the praise line. Sure, not every idea or act is worthy of praise. Yet there's a difference between giving an honest assessment and just being a negative nag. In a desperate attempt to soothe darkness within, some people make themselves feel better by mocking the famous (or more famous). Schoolyard social dynamics are used to boost egos or generate a laugh at the expense of others.

Even with authorized photos, there's still a lot you can't control. Erroneous information isn't limited to trashy tabloids. Respected news organizations like CNN have been lax in their fact checking, as evidenced from time to time on their bottom screen crawl.

You have to have a thick skin to stand whole against what is essentially bullying. Show grace under pressure. Show class and rise above the crass. Detach from the gossip, good and bad. Caring about being judged is akin to being in competition with yourself—but according to the standards of others. Be accountable for and deal with the consequences of your words. Don't invite yourself to be mocked mercilessly through overboard or entitled behavior. If you don't want to be bashed, don't bash others. You may be just a step away from your own fall from grace. I'm sure you don't want to see your unkind remarks reflected back upon you.

Believe in yourself. It's very tempting to browse the media to search for news and innuendo about your personal life. By all means, keep track of what your fans and the media think of you, but don't let that influence what you think of yourself. If you're publicist is doing his job, he will be on top of the thread about you even if you'd rather not bring that process into your daily routine.

Many high-profile people tend to forget that, before all the hype, before all the public attention and adulation came, there was the will of the person who made it all possible. You are more than what the media thinks of you, and you are no less than what you think of yourself.

While many tabloid stories are pure fiction, it's very tough to sue a publication. You have to prove malice and negligence. While some file defamation claims and win, the legal pursuit drew more attention to the incendiary story.

Crying foul only adds fuel to the friction. Hiding behind your various social media profiles to hit back just turns what might have been a single remark into a global viral chorus of verbal assault. Take the high road. It will get you to where you want to end up. Always.

The Reality of Reality TV

The system can't be beat—no matter who you are—if you want to keep the job.
                                    – Aviva Drescher

Being on a Reality TV show is the golden ticket to fame and fortune. The unknown now have the potential to become household names and secure opportunities that would otherwise be merely a dream. In today's reality-television saturated market, there seems to be a show about anything and everything. The more conflicted, comical or sexy the characters, the better. Susan Simons, a veteran agent at David Shapira and Associates (DSA), told me: "Nobody wants clean, good, mild, or calm. They want crazy characters. That's what it takes to create a reality show with legs to last." Nobody cares about philanthropy or do-gooder shows.

Certainly there are benefits to be had with a coveted placement on such a show. If nothing else, it's a well paying gig while it lasts. There are also risks. Divorces and bankruptcies are frequent side effects. Spending tends to surpass income beyond the revenue spike of the show's one or two seasons. Keeping up appearances or false visions of an endless flow of moneymaking opportunities serve as encouragement to buy more without actually earning more.

The outcomes aren't bad for everyone. Several real housewives have cashed in—big time. Many have been able to launch their own businesses as a result of their public exposure. Real Housewife of New York City Bethany Frankel is perhaps the savviest at leveraging her notoriety, and she's earned millions. She's publicly stated that she went on the show single-handedly and exclusively for business. Her

Skinnygirl cocktail line was rapidly embraced by fans, leading to an acquisition by the world's fourth largest spirits company, Fortune Brands' Beam Global, for a price tag reported anywhere from $100-120 million. Her time on the show was a sound business proposition.

Proving that there's no business like show business, Frankel continues to build her entrepreneurial empire that includes liquor, fashion, nutrition lines, best-selling fiction and non-fiction books, and a new television shows. Her marriage, though, didn't survive. The drama around Frankel's highly publicized split with husband Jason Hoppy became a reality show of sorts, as the media and the masses ran play-by-play commentary.

Many others witnessed a significant uptick in their business growth as a direct result of their television appearances. Top Chefs Fabio Viviani and Richard Blais say multiple broadcast experiences were a boon for their business, enabling an unprecedented level of growth. Even though the exposure delivered greater awareness, there was still a lot of hard work involved in maintaining the advancements.

Any person involved with reality television programs knows one thing: Reality TV drama shows aren't real. They're largely influenced or outright fabricated entertainment by producers made for the mass consumption. Producers shape shows to attract the biggest audience and the most advertising dollars. They want dramatic and controversial personalities and encourage emotional outbursts. Those who can bait fellow participants to act out become indispensible. When the reality becomes boring, "real" situations are edited to twist reality.

Sarah Austin, one of the stars of Bravo's *Start-Ups: Silicon Valley*, believes the need for entertaining drama placed her in a position where she had to constantly defend herself on the show. She always felt pressured to defend and deny rumors and accusations thrown at her by other show participants. Looking back on her experience, Austin wished she had prepared by taking acting classes so she could better play a character that was the best version of herself!

Competition between the stars for camera face time adds pressure. Entertainment comes from conflict, so producers stitch it together in a crazy quilt: mixing timelines, reactions, and conversations to fit the script of the drama. Fans love or hate the characters on the show for reasons regularly based on creative editing rather than reality.

If you agreed to participate in a reality show pilot, did you know what you were getting into? Did you even know the name of the show you signed up for? Were you astute enough to get an agent or attorney to explain how little control over your individual story arc you have? Even though you were earning a salary as a cast member, were you aware that you'll be picking up your own tab for the lavish dinners and parties you'll be attending and hosting on the show? It's easy to get in over your head financially when trying to keep up with the expectations of the show producers and the bar set by other cast members.

If you thought you could stay true to your real life story, including the way you typically relate to others, you were in for a big surprise. Real people don't exist in sanitized, prepackaged, single-serving episodes. Viewers want outrageous characters and drama, not the ordinary routine that fills so much of a normal day in a normal life. Producers format and plot the shows before filming even begins to ensure the story and drama happens.

In my talks with reality show stars, they report they were least prepared for the pressures and problems their families and loved ones took on for them. Many family members want nothing to do with the fictional story or the attention of the media seeking "the real story behind the scenes."

Some shows actively exploit family drama to sell shows. Constant pressure for drama and scripted "authentic" moments, combined with non-stop exposure, creates problems between friends, couples, and families. A strong discipline and commitment to your personal relationships throughout filming will enable them to endure after the show ends.

In the perpetual schedule of taping, the on-screen persona overpowers the real person who takes off her camera-ready make-up at night. Some stars become a bit schizophrenic by the frequent change of masks between an on-screen persona, their public image as they blog or tweet about the show, and their talk show interview personality. Somewhere behind all those masks lies the "real" person—who may be lost forever.

If that happens, you'll become known as the manufactured version of yourself, and it won't be flattering. To feel confident, secure, and comfortable in the strange land of Reality TV, make sure you're surrounded by an excellent support system to keep you real and on-course during the show and beyond. It will be necessary to require confidentiality agreements with your professional supporters, as you are undoubtedly under strict orders to stay mum about what's going on as you tape the show. Your support team will help you avoid the temptation of being part of the series drama and playing permanently into the fictional persona you're forced to create.

The way you're treated as you travel about your neighborhood, community, country, and globally (if your show is a hit) will change. Some of it shifts for the better. Some of it will make you feel like an alien. People you knew before the show will suddenly act differently with you. Strangers will stare or address you as if they know you personally. The TV-watching-public has no idea how to respond when encountering a celebrity of any kind. Their models are the media and paparazzi, who do nothing but hound stars, so this behavior becomes "normal." Privacy for a reality TV star is nearly impossible, especially during the airing of the show season. Even more distressing is the tape delay. The public rarely recognizes that events that played on their television last night may have happened to you months ago, resolved and settled between cast members. To them, it happened yesterday. Private lives become public, and labels stick whether they reflect reality or not.

I've had the pleasure of knowing and working quite a few Reality TV stars in one capacity or another. Over a quiet dinner at one of my favorite restaurants, The Strand in Manhattan Beach, CA, Mary Amons (former star of *Real Housewives, D.C.*) told me how she came to the realization that despite her intention to 'be real' on the show, what she allowed the cameras to see was only a small glimpse of what was going on in her very real world. While it was true that Amons was an active mother of five, wife of a successful businessman, and a dedicated philanthropist, the audience (as well as the crew) never saw that the marriage was less than its perfect presentation. The truth was, it was barely managing to tread in its very troubled waters.

Realizing her own betrayal of her promise to herself to "be real," Amons realized she was denying who she was underneath the labels of mother, wife, and philanthropist. What made up the fiber of her being, the fabric of her life as an individual? The truth was, she wasn't so sure anymore about who she was and what she wanted.

That wake up call led Amons on a journey of self-actualization that now directs her life. The show gave her an audience that is still engaged today and a platform to expand her ability to do more good in the world. Amons is now relieved that the show didn't get picked up for a second season because she and her family were released from all contractual obligations to Bravo. She's free to create her future as she pleases. One of the greatest gifts her celebrity status gives her is the chance to meet a lot of interesting people from all walks of life, who she feels are far more interesting than their interest in her.

When asked what advice she'd give to others stepping up to the Reality TV experience, Amons offered the following:

- Be yourself.

- Keep your head held high.

- Stay out of the drama as much as possible. It's important to be grounded in your purpose as you jump into the shark tank that is the reality TV experience.

- Contribute in a meaningful and entertaining way.

- Be relaxed and willing to make fun of yourself when you have to blog about each episode.

Kari Wells, featured on Bravo's *Married to Medicine*, advises those who are thinking about becoming a participant on a reality TV show to examine their motives. Take a hard look at why you'd do it. If you're just going for the fame or money, then you really need to take a second look because it's not all fun and games. Every aspect of your life is judged and cruelly criticized. The verbal assault also reaches your family and children, especially through social media. So much can easily be misconstrued and cause a great deal of pain.

Wells expressed to me how frustrating it was not to be able to talk to anyone about what she was experiencing during the grueling and endless days of taping the first season of her show. Under a strict confidentiality agreement with Bravo, Wells couldn't discuss the events and interactions caught on camera. She worried about what would be aired and in what context. She wasn't sure how she'd be portrayed, especially after one episode that ended with two of her fellow cast members getting into a fistfight in the middle formal gathering held at Well's beautiful home. Cameras rolled as Wells said, "We're done. This is over.. Wells was speaking to the show producers. When the episode aired, it appeared that she was addressing her party guests.

Aviva Drescher was torn in her choice to accept the offer to become part of the cast of *Real Housewives of New York*. She said it was one of the most difficult choices she's had to make in her life. Like Amons and Wells, Drescher thought the exposure would give her a unique experience. She'd have a front-row seat and a backstage pass to pop culture. The show offered her an opportunity and a platform to draw attention to the causes she supports and expand her ability to do more for her philanthropic pursuits, especially for those who are physically challenged.

Drescher thought she knew what she was getting into. She'd seen the drama unfold in other reality shows and thought she'd be portrayed as the voice of reason, as she is in her real life. She was certain she wouldn't become *bat shit crazy* like she'd seen in the behavior of many reality show stars. She was confident that she would be able to stay above the fray, and people would see her civilized self.

At the worst, she'd be seen as boring.

What she didn't realize is that there's a formula to reality show programming, and if you don't play the game, you're out. Even though she didn't handle the on screen drama as she hoped, Drescher was appalled to see the cartoon character she'd become through the production process and a heavy dose of editing. Instead of being the centered soul of the group, she was seen as the top of the bat shit crazy chart.

What she learned from the experience is that she couldn't get invested in the positive things people said about her presence on the show. Drescher didn't want to get an unrealistic "big head." She also learned that she couldn't allow herself to be brought down by the negative naysayers. She learned that she had to become bullet-proof. She'd witness other cast members become overly influenced by public reaction to the point where they betray friendships, values, and (occasionally) reason. At the end of the day, everyone wants to be liked, and it's very hard to maintain likeability within the framework of reality television production.

If reality television is part of your reality, go into it with open eyes and sound intentions. Be the author instead of the character of the persona portrayed on screen. While the role is a version of the real you, shape the role authentically based upon the brand you wish to build, and you'll benefit from it long after the final credits roll. Don't allow your public persona, no matter how large it is, to overshadow the person who you really are, leaving its image as an external caricature of the person you truly are.

If you think landing a part as a cast member on a reality show will serve as a launch pad for additional television opportunities, think again. If a reality show is your only television experience, you really don't have any leverage, unless you were the one that really stood out in a big way. If so, agents and producers will gravitate to you and lock you up in a contract immediately—for more Reality TV.

Discovering, recommitting to, and fully aligning with your why is one of the key differentiators between a celebrity who recognizes his or herself in the mirror each morning, feels fulfilled, and is inspired to continue growing and enriching from the inside out. Why do you do what you do? *Really*. Something somewhere hidden deep in your past made your heart skip a beat, and at that pivotal moment, you imagined your destiny. The journey may have led you on some unexpected and unimaginable paths, but the call within your heart remained. In that drive was a practical and emotional purpose that would return you to that feeling of awe, inspiration, and pure joy.

Titillating temptations beacon you to distraction daily. What appear to be bright, shiny objects of desire fade into wayward diversions that cloud your ultimate dream. Intuition loses out to justification. Rationalization's song and dance leads you astray like the lure of a siren.

It's not about what you do; it's why you do it. What is your *raison d'être*? It's the question to be asked of yourself and of every choice you make, personally and professionally. Whenever you feel lost, frustrated, or uncertain, get out of your head and into your heart. Ask yourself: "Why am I here?" Burning within you is a curiosity that keeps asking you that question. Only you can answer it, and answer it you must. Otherwise, you'll have no anchor, and you'll be set adrift, crashing against the waves until your opportunities are shipwrecked forever.

When you get a bead on your purpose, answering the ultimate question of life your choices and decisions from that day forward are much easier. Your *Why* becomes the central motivation that explains everything you do. It will remind you to stay true to your passion long after the initial inspiration wanes.

Your intuition, the voice of your heart, will serve as your personal GPS guiding you at every turn, roadblock, or fork in the road. Your *Why* isn't something you merely tell yourself and others. Be the living expression and demonstration of your *Why*. It is what will keep you on track.

I won't lie to you and say keeping your *Why* top of mind is easy-peasy. It's not. It takes discipline to remind yourself to honor and consistently stay connected with your *Why*. For those who do, the payoff can be huge. It delivers the pure feeling that you, life, and living in this world is truly awesome. And you, by your presence and purpose, made a meaningful difference. Ultimately, at the end of your days, fulfillment comes from the fullest expression and realization of your *Why*.

As you might have imagined from the above, the other key differentiator between those who deftly ride the dragon of fame and those who get stomped upon by it is how you exercise your *power of choice*.

Chapter Four
Maintain the Flame

A lot of the problems I had with fame I was bringing on myself. A lot of self-loathing and a lot of woe-is-me. Now I'm learning to see the positive side of things instead of, "I can't go to Kmart. I can't take my kids to the haunted house."

– *Eminem*

Wealth is like seawater; the more we drink, the thirstier we become; and the same is true of fame.
— *Arthur Schopenhauer*

I think all of us are 5-year-olds and we don't want to be embarrassed in the schoolyard.

— *Helen Hunt*

Staying Ahead of the Fire

As challenging as it is to get there, it can be even more challenging to stay there. Whether you signed up for it or not, you're on the ultimate treadmill endurance test. Demanding and difficult workloads, long hours, life lived under the transparent lights of the media, and relentless public scrutiny wears heavily upon your patience, upon your soul.

Fame, success, and wealth can be erratic and fleeting. Things will change. Life is a series of changes. There's really only one thing more important than change and that's the ability to be completely comfortable in it. Fame can change your life, but it doesn't have to change you. Maintaining the flame depends upon the strength of your conviction.

Have you been to an artist's studio? We're not talking here about a successful and well-known painter. No, our artist is not yet famous, but she is very passionate about her work. She paints every day in her studio despite not having had an opening exhibition or sold many paintings.

If you have visited such an artist's studio, you will be amazed at the way the paintings are stacked haphazardly, with no regard for form or order. They are everywhere. Completed canvases are leaning against the walls and those that are in progress are standing on easels. There's hardly any room to move around. You are afraid that you will knock over something if you make a wrong turn. You look around, and you don't know where to look. There's as much clutter as there are colors.

A few months later, the artist has her first ever exhibition and you receive an invitation. At the art gallery, you see the very same paintings that you saw lying around in her studio a few months earlier arranged neatly on the walls. Adorning each painting is a frame and a halo from a spotlight. There are valleys of empty white space on the wall separating each painting from the next.

This is where the paintings belong, you think: in the expansive interiors of the gallery rather than in a dinky little studio.

As a famous personality, when you are on stage, whether it is real or metaphorical, in the midst of your fans and admirers, you feel this is where you belong.

I invite you to consider a different perspective.

Standing in the art gallery, in the midst of a crowd of admirers, you eavesdrop on the compliments and the criticisms and wonder if these people would have said the same things had they seen these same paintings huddled together in her studio like you did a few months back? Perhaps some of them with a discerning eye would have, but you are sure most of them wouldn't. You were not much impressed yourself, you remember, when you first saw the same paintings in the studio.

You cannot help but wonder how the artist feels about seeing her work in a gallery. Does she see the difference? You look at the artist standing unassumingly and then you suddenly realize that she cannot afford to look at her work any differently, whether it is in a cramped and cluttered studio or in the spacious environs of a gallery. Her work is insulated from external influences. It has to be.

You cannot expect the artist to put an empty canvas in a gilded frame, put a spotlight on it, and start filling it with colors. No, a painting starts taking form on an easel in surroundings whose relative influence is marginal. The painter, when she is working, is oblivious to her surroundings, whether it is in a studio, on the beach, in a busy shopping mall, or in a quiet gallery. The painting takes shape from within. Of course, she may be looking at a subject in front of her, a model or a still life, but the expression that is applied on the canvas comes from within the artist.

When you are famous, you think you have been transformed.

You are—if you see things from a distance, through the eyes of your fans and admirers, as an outsider. You are not if you are looking at yourself from within. You exist not because you are famous. You are famous because of how you exist. A painting is beautiful not because it has a beautiful frame around it and a spotlight on it. It is beautiful because the artist poured her heart and soul into it. It will be beautiful even without the frame and the spotlight.

Stay intuitively connected with your inner compass and the conviction that set you off on this path at the very beginning. When fame takes you on a voyage, your sense of direction is best determined by the real you rather than the public persona that other people think is you. As any sailor will tell you, the figurehead on the front of a ship is just for show, what really matters is the rudder. That's how you steer your ship in the direction you want it to go.

To continue the metaphor, while the surface of the sea may look the same as you travel, what lies beneath constantly changes. The sky above you transitions from day to night and through various weather patterns. While all this change is going on, you still keep your route well mapped as you steadily move forward. Most of the changes you will go through occur beneath the surface, from within you. You change how you deal with the demands, expectations, and pressure of your day-to-day life. You may shift your desires and goals. Your external experience is merely a reflection of the changes going on inside of you. Your body will change as you age, yet you are still you. Hopefully, with each passing day you become a more empowered and expanded version of the person who is reading these words today.

Change doesn't happen in a cacophony of noise and activity. It happens in the quiet rests between the pulse beats of living. A spark, an intuition, an "Ah-ha!" moment reveals itself. As a result, energy shifts. When your energy shifts, how and who you are being is transformed. The transition creates a different direction, resulting in a new outcome, a change in the *status quo*.

Hit the Pause Button

When adversity strikes, that's when you have to be the most calm. Take a step back, stay strong, stay grounded and press on.

– LL Cool J

The subject of choices is mentioned throughout the book because it is the other key differentiator between those who deftly ride the dragon of fame and those who get stomped upon by it. How you exercise your *power of choice* is the partner and co-joined twin to your *Why*. You can't authoritatively choose unless you're present, awake, and aware. You can't choose something better unless you're aware of what you're choosing.

Fame is devilish. It can play chicken with your sanity. Your rational self can buckle under the pressure to become an irrational distortion of you, warping your ability to make choices that serve your highest interests. The more your life becomes fast-paced and high-pressured, the more you are likely to cope by defaulting to impulsive or habitual reactions instead of through a mindful decision based on the following foundation:

- Which choice will help me become the highest version of myself that I can possibly be?

- Which choice is aligned closest to what I value most?

- Which choice is an act of faith rather than fear?

- Which choice will enrich instead of drain my energy?

In a fast-paced, high-pressure life, it's easy to miss the choices in front of you. Instead of being awake and alert in your experience, you're asleep at the proverbial wheel, unaware of the choices you make.

In a reactive mode (vs. decisive) we all get "triggered" and respond with a knee-jerk reaction instead of a carefully considered choice. Reactions are not fixed or immutable. You have the power to change how you receive the affairs of your life any time you choose. How you navigate the events of your life shapes and defines the content and quality of your character. The 10/90 Principle states that 10% of life is made up of what happens to you—90% of life is decided by how you react to those events. Deliberate choice in alignment with your highest potential is the path to freedom. Ultimately, your decisions dictate your destiny.

The ability to hit the pause button, to mindfully act instead of unconsciously react is what separates the ordinary from the extraordinary. It gives you a chance to further develop and strengthen your emotional intelligence. Envision the bigger picture for every decision you make. You can direct your life unconsciously on autopilot or consciously in control of the steering wheel. You want to drive (rather than be run over by your circumstance). If you're awake and aware, you can hit the pause button any time you choose. Giving yourself a moment to think enables you to mindfully direct your experiences instead of blindly reacting as life's victim.

This is especially true when it comes to social media. Think before you tweet or react to a media story. Drinking and tweeting is never a good idea. Period. For that matter, drinking excessively anywhere close to a camera or anything that can record your behavior is profoundly unwise. This is to say, don't do it anywhere, even in your own home. There have been incidents where family members, employees, or friends are the ones who betray privacy—even if unwittingly.

Life happens for you, not to you. There is meaning and purpose in every experience. Your job is to figure out what it is. Taking the time to discern where you are and where you want to go gives you the power to orchestrate the outcome you wish to achieve.

Inner chaos creates outer chaos. Hitting the pause button also gives you a chance to replenish and restore harmony. When life becomes overwhelming or you feel drained, take a time out. Renew your resources by doing something that feeds your soul. I'm not necessarily talking about taking care of your body, such as a deep tissue massage or mani-pedi. What's most needed and wanted is what will catapult you back into the zone refueled by passion and inspiration. If a spa day is what works for you, great. But if it means going to a concert or seeing an exhibition or taking a week in Honolulu, make the space you need to get back to work effectively.

While the melodious notes of life are resplendent, it is the pauses between the refrains that make them music. Appreciation is found in the silent moments of our awareness. The word "*appreciate*" means both to value and to increase the value of a thing. What we appreciate appreciates. It is impossible to appreciate who you are and what you have if, as Jackson Browne famously noted, you're "running on empty, running blind, running into the sun." You probably already know just how crazy that life feels.

Reject Rejection

Sometimes I feel my whole life has been one big rejection.

– Marilyn Monroe

You've chosen a trajectory littered with opportunities that invite rejection. To be human is to know rejection, so remind yourself that you're not alone when it comes to feeling the pain of repudiation. What gives rise to the most hurtful of hurts is when a dismissal of you in the context of an opportunity is internalized as a rejection of you as a human being. No one can reject you as a person without your permission. You have to buy into the brush-off or thumbs down of your value as an individual. Learn how to take a bullet well. Don't let your failures define you. Allow them to refine you.

While you have credits to show for the work you've done, you're still in a very competitive industry. Lots of people want the same things you want. While yours is unique, there's a lot of talent and smarts out there that rival yours. It may be awhile before you can consistently get work merely on the strength of your name.

If you audition for a role and are told to find another career, this is not a rejection of you and your passion. It's just one person's opinion. Executives rejected Charlie Chaplin because they thought his act was too obscure for people to understand. They got it wrong. Marilyn Monroe was told she wasn't pretty or talented enough to be an actress. She kept plugging away anyway. Even if you completely blew, it give yourself a break. Everyone is in the business of being human, having flaws, and making mistakes. No one is alone. Besides, until you're cracked open, you don't know what you're made of.

If your manuscript is rejected, it's not about you. Twelve publishers famously rejected the best selling author J.K. Rowling book before *Harry Potter and The Philosopher's Stone* was accepted by Bloomsbury. The publisher accepted the book only at the insistence of the chairman's eight-year-old daughter.

If your script ends up in the circular file time and time again, keep pitching and writing. Walt Disney was fired by a newspaper editor because he "lacked imagination had had no good ideas."

If the audience boos, you keep showing up. The first time Jerry Seinfeld went onstage, the crowds jeered. He went on to become one of the most famous comics with one of the most-loved sitcoms ever.

After his first film, the producer told Harrison Ford that he'd probably never succeed. Today, he is one of the highest grossing actors of all time. A favorite of directors Steven Spielberg and George Lucas, Ford is perhaps best known for his iconic roles as Hans Solo and Indiana Jones.

Lucille Ball spent many years lingering on the B-list. Her agent told her to find a new career. She went on to star in *I Love Lucy* and became a top television executive. Her groundbreaking work paved the way for future stars such as Mary Tyler Moore, Penny Marshall, Cybill Shepherd, and Robin Williams.

Oprah Winfrey was fired from her television-reporting job because she wasn't fit to be on screen. She went on to become the undisputed queen of television talk shows seen, on screens of every kind around the world.

Steven Spielberg got rejected from The University of Southern California School of Cinematic Arts three times. That didn't stop this multiple Academy Award winning director, screenwriter, producer, and studio entrepreneur. He took an unpaid, seven-day-a-week, internship at the Universal studios editing department to hone his skills. Once he achieved his extraordinary success, USC invited Spielberg back to accept an honorary degree. Spielberg has since donated funds to the school to help future generations of filmmakers learn and master their craft.

If you're easily dissuaded by rejection then your drive is motivated by all the wrong reasons. There's no passion that fuels your spirit in your motivation. It's okay to indulge in a solitary pissed-off pity-party when things don't go the way you want. Feel what you feel. Release the energy of your emotion. Make no decisions or engage in any important conversations while you're in this funk. They will only drive you deeper into the painful abyss. Once you've processed the pain of rejection, reconnect thoroughly with your *Why* and step up to the plate swinging again and again and again. It's only a matter of time before you hit the ball out of the proverbial park.

Become a Fear Wrangler

Never say never, because limits, like fear, are often an illusion.

– *Michael Jordan*

Fame brings with it abundance in terms of wealth, power, and even moments of pure happiness. Yet if you are not able to enjoy the fruits of being famous, then it's an indication that you are constantly worried and anxious that you don't deserve it. The adulation and the love of fans that you may have once found extremely gratifying start to become a source of irritation, mistrust, and loneliness. Those feelings lead to fear. Yet everyday you have to make decisions about who and what to trust. Never let your fear decide your fate. Any decision made from the emotion of fear or self-doubt will not have a good outcome. Choices rooted in inspiration and intuition will spirit you onward in a positive direction.

Here are three tips to manage fear:

1. Discern the Feeling

The SIN of fear is that our "Self-Inflicted Nonsense" usually creates it. What is it, exactly, that frightens you? Is it an all-consuming fear that grips your gut, requiring immediate action to mitigate danger or is it based on a more mysterious concern about what lies in wait for you beyond your comfort zone? Distinguishing the nuances of your fear gives you a foundation within which to deal with it effectively.

Your emotions are indicators of whether or not you're thinking in a direction that serves you or diminishes you. Simply put, if you feel good, you're headed in the right direction. Move forward. If you feel bad, stop. Take a moment to breathe. Discern whether or not what you fear is real and imminent. What is the evidence that the fear or immediacy is real? Is there any evidence to the contrary? Examine the facts without attaching any emotion or imposed meanings, tuning out all the inner chatter about the veracity of the situation. If the fear is real and/or imminent, take rational and appropriate precautions. If it isn't, release your fear as you would the handles of your baggage when the hotel porter takes them from you upon your arrival.

2. Trust Your Inner Circle

Keep your inner circle close. These are people you love, know, like, and trust. Because they know, like, and trust you, they serve as a safety net to cushion any fall. Communicate and spend time with them often. Allow yourself to be open and transparent in their presence. Use them as sounding boards and allow them to reflect new perspectives. Seeing your world through a new landscape will move the stagnant energy in your mind. Reach for the viewpoint that makes you feel better and more capable of dealing with whatever it is you fear.

3. Reconnect With You

Often the most profound feelings of fear are the result of a disconnection from your authentic self. As a celebrity, you spend a lot of time in your public persona "costume." The flip side of that coin is you begin to lose touch with who you really are underneath the façade. You start to play 'what if' scenarios in your head that threaten vulnerability, possibility of loss, or humiliation. Most of what people fear never comes true. It's the dark night of the soul that keeps us up at night, not the reality of what it is we're so afraid.

The extraordinary create and live life on the raw and ragged edge. Your ability to move beyond the boundaries of your fear will get better with practice. Remember to breathe. The more you apply these three steps, the more you will feel like you belong and are fully connected to the fabric and vibrancy of life at its fullest.

Be Your Own Showrunner

Sometimes you can have the smallest role in the smallest production and still have a big impact.
– Neil Patrick Harris

Your life is not a work of fiction, no matter how outlandish or far from reality the events that happen to you and around you. What happens is not coincidence but events triggered by your actions or your reactions. Take charge and mindfully direct what happens in the story of your life. Don't let a stray wind blow away the pages. It's not just a few pages that are being turned. It's some of the best years of your life. Enjoy and live them to their highest potential.

Know who's pulling the strings. It's you. Not your fans or your entourage. You are the main actor in the movie of your life, so be its playwright and director as well. The show may revolve around you but the world doesn't. So be worthy of your role in the show and don't believe in, much less start living, the hype.

When you're on a journey, you will see signs that reveal what lies ahead in each direction. You'll also meet people who tell you where they've been and why you should or should not go there. Some of these people are what I call the should-ers. They will *should* all over you to shape you into their view of the world and what is right. Appreciate the sharing of information as you keep your eyes and ears open. Look, listen, and decide for yourself where you want to go and at what pace you want to travel.

Refer to your inner compass when in doubt. The direction will have a good outcome if you have a good feeling when you are inspired to make such a move. You'll not like where you end up if the choice was made out of fear or doubt. It's really as simple as that. Your emotions are remarkable indicators of whether you're headed in a direction that will serve or diminish you. Pay attention and you'll never lose your way.

Be genuine. Know who you are and acknowledge the gifts that you possess. At the same time, be aware of the dangers of wandering too far from the range of your perceptive powers. If you happen to find yourself adrift in unfamiliar waters, it's time to focus, not panic, and get reconnected with your inner resources. That's why it is important to stay aligned with what you value most and be among people and things that keep you grounded in reality.

When you interact with the people in the community, you are forming a connection with them. Your existence becomes linked to this public persona. This is where the lines between who you really are and who your fans or admirers want to be merge. The dream of celebrity can quickly become a nightmare if you try to constantly to meet the expectations of fans.

When you're living in a fishbowl, where your every move is exposed, then you are liable to become a victim of *celebrity-bashing* masses who, like bullies in the sandbox, throw sand in your face and kick you when you're down or vulnerable. The blogs, magazines, and celebrity news in all platforms are atwitter about the latest riches-to-rags, high-on-life to high-on-drugs and from diamond bracelets to handcuffs story. It's become an expected story, even about the most unexpected people. Yes, given the unrelenting pressure of popularity, it can happen to you. There are plenty of frequent reminders of those who fall through the trap door of a misguided escape from it all.

Of course, the demands and expectations are often unfair. You never asked to be objectified, demoralized, controlled, deceived, bought, sold, and live in a gilded cage where everything looks beautiful from the outside but from the inside you wish some or all of it would go away. No more bad hair days allowed. No more relaxing walks or visits to your favorite public places. No more security. You assume only the worst about the true motivations behind an offer of friendship and support.

How could those who love you suddenly turn against you and berate you for no fault of yours? You wonder. Fame lifts its middle finger of fate and can quickly point it at you. That's why. It's nothing personal. Fame's just a schizophrenic bitch. However you look at it, there are many sides to her genres of comedy, tragedy, drama, and documentary.

What you say and what you do is a reflection of who you are. There is no script to follow. There are no lines to memorize. There's only your own true self to rely upon. You're not what the media has created but a real person with original thoughts and sentiments. Express them with verve, live according to your standards, make your own rules, and don't be afraid to follow them. Here are a few thoughts to get you going.

Be kind, compassionate, and authentic. Before you speak in the public arena check to make sure what you're about to say is benevolent, true, and necessary. Dr. Seuss reminded you as a child that you could say what you mean, mean what you say, without being mean. That one simple tip will keep you out of a lot of hot water.

Embrace the personal acknowledgment by your fans, even if they interrupt your dinner. Spend at least thirty seconds expressing your appreciation for their support before you excuse yourself to go back to your conversation. Without fans that invest in your career through buying what your brand produces, you wouldn't have much equity in your star power. Receive your public as you would like to be received.

Make room for media in your life, but live your life with verity. Let others conjure up the illusions. Enjoy them but don't believe them. Remain true to you core values, as they give form to your notions.

When you don't agree with something someone says or does—and especially if you are in the eye of the media—breathe for a beat or two before you utter a sound. Think before you talk. Make sure your words are necessary, kind, true, and an improvement upon the silence.

Think before you leap. A moment to allow clarity to surface never fails to put things in perspective. Just a few moments are all you usually need to collect your thoughts and find your bearings to make the right decisions say and do the right things.

You're not an idol that can be shattered. You're a real person. Even if the idol breaks, you don't. If someone tries to break your image, they are not breaking you, just the vision they have of you. Maintain that perspective. Listen to advice and feedback as you discern what is in your highest interests.

Remain humble. To be famous is to belong to an exclusive club, you get to rub shoulders with the other elite, but that doesn't mean you have to trade in your values. One way to tell if you're aligned with your core values is to take a look at your credit card statement. Is what you're spending the bulk of your money on what you value most? If so, you're getting a tremendous return of fulfillment on those investments. If not, it's never to late to make some changes. It's a simple check-in I recommend be exercised frequently.

Keep your cool. If you're no longer enjoying the ride, if you feel anxious and things start moving too fast for comfort, slow down. Stop. Adjust what needs adjusting. It's your life, so you get to determine its pace, temperature, and substance.

It's one thing to feel proud of your achievements. It's another to feel indignant that someone else doesn't acknowledge them in the way you desire. There will be times when you are tempted to say, "Do you know who I am?" At times like these, ask yourself: would you ask a mirror the question? Who are you really trying to impress? The answer will be you. Who you are being will always speak louder than what you are labeled.

Shine on, you crazy diamond.

Keep Your Feet on the Ground

I think anybody who's famous has to deal with fame in their own way, and I dealt with it by making a film about a kid who's looking out into the world of celebrity obsession.

– Adrian Grenier

People become famous for many different reasons. Some trade in their soul for a wish. If absolute power corrupts absolutely, so does absolute fame. It's easy to lose perspective when your identity is wrapped up in stardom. If you find yourself playing the *I'm better, more important, and more special than the little people* game, then get off your high falutin' perch and put your feet back on the ground.

No matter how much fame, money, power, free stuff, or sex you have, you are still human like everyone else. You still bleed. You can be hurt. You experience joy as well as pain. You want to be loved. There are parts of your inner journey that still confront and confound you. And, like everyone, you will die one day. The answer to the exasperated accusation of *don't you know who I am?* is often *yes, just a guy acting like a jerk*. If you want to be valued, start by valuing others—including their needs, time, and service.

While you may be able to play the celebrity card to your advantage, you aren't perfect. No one is. And why would you want to be? If you're perfect, there's no room for growth, learning, or creativity. Might as well call it a day on this life.

Models of grounded stars are abundant. Academy Award winners Tom Hanks, Ron Howard, Meryl Streep, Octavia Spencer, and (hard to believe it's only) nominee Johnny Depp are just a few

143

examples. Beyoncé says changing diapers keeps her grounded. Emily Blunt does her own dishes. Brad Pitt credits Gwyneth Paltrow's father for helping to keep him grounded. Patrow taught him to consider himself *employed* rather than *an actor*. For Pitt, working for a living is a humble reminder of what he does. Halle Berry remembers the night in 2002 when she won the Academy Award for best actress. Driving home that night, she felt like Cinderella. Berry reminded herself that when the night was over, she'd go back to who she really is. And she did.

Notoriety should not be confused with fame. By all means, listen to what your publicist advises, but also listen to what your heart tells you. Only your highest self, expressed through your intuition and inspiration, knows what's in your best interests. Discern the difference between the voice of your potential and the voice of your fear. The former will make you feel alive and energized; the latter will trigger a freeze, flee, or fight impulse.

Be grounded in your humility and connected by your humanity. Be compassionate in your outlook of how the media creates stories. It's not about you. It's about getting eyeballs to advertising. Whenever you hear negative stories, remember that whatever the media is doing is not out of spite. But it is in the nature of the media to exploit negative stories because the Schadenfreude nature of the public demands it. Beyond those who know and love you personally, very few really care about whether you enjoy long-term success or not, including your fans. The general public revels when you fall because it generally redeems their personal perceived pitfalls and failures.

The boulevard of fame is littered with the shadows of forgotten celebrities. Among these shadows, you will also notice celebrities whom age and time have treated well. Those who've aged gracefully in the spotlight are emulated. Be among them.

It's possible to keep your feet firmly planted in the foundation of reality while your shadow plays with the magic and power of celebrity and influence. Your humility and humanity will keep you on *terra firma* even as your fame soars. It's an irony that the Walk of Fame is considered an honor by many stars. It is coveted ground, literally littered with stars—and anyone can walk all over them.

While celebrity, money, and connections can provide access to additional resources and opportunities, it guarantees you nothing. Too many have tried all the wrong ways to fill the void between who they are and who they want to be through believing in their own hype, elite hobnobbing, luxury purchases, and living *la vida loca*.

Give yourself permission to slow things down from time to time. Allow yourself a chance to enjoy each moment, develop along spiritual lines that are useful for you. Instead of trying to balance your life, reach for harmony in your quest for equilibrium in how you invest your time. After you've spent endless days, weeks, or months devoted to a particular project schedule down time to enjoy a little quiet time to renew your sense of inner peace.

The enemy of your good fortune is within and lives by the name of self-sabotage. Many smart accomplished people worked hard at making a lot of money and even harder at losing it. Actor Charlie Sheen may have "won" the throne of most bizarre poster boy status in this category, but he shares his reign with a lot of other people. In addition to his booze and drug abuse, his over-the-top bad boy behavior resulted in expensive divorces while derailing his career. One very public rampage of multiple temper tantrums got him tossed off the set of the top television series in which he starred. That one event cost him (and those involved with the show) tens of millions of dollars.

Regarding his criticized behavior, Sheen makes a point that deserves respect and recognition. When he says, "I'm not anything like you people." He's right. The average person wasn't born into a famous family. Sheen's dad is, of course, the well-known actor Martin Sheen. Sheen will never face the typical problems of "everyday" people. He won't have to worry about how to keep a roof over his head. He'll always have enough money for the basic necessities of an average comfortable life, at the very least. He has resources, opportunities, and connections available to him that the "normal" man or woman works a lifetime to cultivate, often falling short. In that context, Sheen is not like most people and resents being judged through that lens.

He has, however, a different set of problems and challenges that are often part of the package when you're born as the son of a high-profile father. He was also born an heir to the Sheen estate. I've written at length in one of my earlier books, *Money Moxie: How to Transcend the Paradox of Privilege and Liberate Your True Worth*, about the unique struggles experienced by children who grow up in wealthy and/or prominent families. While society may give short shrift to such difficulties, they are very real.

Some famous personalities, like Neil Patrick Harris, Beyoncé, and Emeril Lagasse, thrive in their success. Others are wrecked by it. Why is that?

Some people fall apart when they achieve huge success. Robert Downey, Jr. is a guy who had it all and then threw it all away in a sea of self-sabotage that included drug abuse, arrests for trespassing, gun charges, and a yearlong prison sentence. In an Oscar-worthy inspirational true story, Downey transformed his misspent life into becoming a poster child of redemption and a remarkable life well-lived.

Drew Barrymore made a stunning transition from being a washed-out child-star on a path of self-ruination to an award-winning highly recognized power in Hollywood. She discovered that life experiences are not events that happen to you but are the direct result of choices made. This new way of thinking about her past experience and what she wanted to create for her future was the result of a shift from "I am a victim of my circumstances" to "I have the power to create the life I want to experience." She moved from being a troubled child born into a dysfunctional yet famous Hollywood Family, destined to recreate the same destructive life for herself that her mother experienced, to taking deliberate charge of her own personal and professional choices.

If you are one of the many people who think money or fame has the power to make the inner saboteur vanish, think again. The reality is that your status has no such power. If your ego is undernourished with what it needs most (and can't be purchased), it will devour your success and damage everything else in its path.

Believe at your deepest core that you're worthy of your achievement and elevated status. Otherwise, you're liable to unconsciously work very hard to return to from where you came. Your energy and attention will be invested in self-doubt rather than your greatest possible future.

Fame brings greater choices, more outer opportunities, and more stages to try out your performance. More choices mean more decisions and therefore more chances of getting it wrong. When trapped, your motives for the choices you make become elusive. You may tell yourself, and even believe, you're acting out of a genuine desire for freedom, security, recognition, comfort, or independence. Too often, those who feel this way unknowingly act in a way they think will make them more comfortable in the gilded cage they've constructed for themselves.

It's scary to dare to live beyond comfort zones and step boldly into the land of vulnerability. This is the home of **f.e.a.r.** You'll know its presence when you *find excuses and reasons* for your behavior or want to *fuck everything and run* away or into whatever will serve as your security blanked. Like shots of Tequila, these things are better used in small doses. Instead, face the challenges with spirit and courage.

Be Human and Humble

*I don't have a set of tenets, but I live an ethical life. I
practice a humility that presupposes there's a power
greater than myself. And I always believe, don't inflict
harm where it's not necessary.*

– Michael J. Fox

A strong ego is a positive attribute and a key brick in the foundation
of success. An unhealthy ego will be its undoing. A well-developed
ego knows when and where to serve itself and when and where to
serve others. Unbridled ego and pride can get you into predicaments
where you feel out of control. A sure sign that you're letting your ego
and pride get inflated is when you find yourself in a frequent state of
foot-in-mouth. Turning bad situations into worse, blaming others, or
denying the truth are also symptoms of an unhealthy perspective.

Egomaniacs, the domineering jerks that don't know when to be
quiet and or away from the cameras, can be entertaining at first. Soon
they become a tiresome presence that is to be avoided at all costs.
The arrogance that accompanies an overblown ego will eventually
undermine the façade of greatness and infallibility. Those who achieve
from the inside out don't feel the need to beat their magnificence into
the public mind. They let their presence and promise speak for itself.

Fat egos feel entitled. You've heard about the stereotypical divas
demanding outrageous hotel accommodations and amenities with
little patience or respect for those who are just trying to do their jobs
well. There was a time when hotels kept such incidents on the hush-
hush to remain in favor with their high-profile guests. With today's
viral videos and social media reach, the unrealistic expectations of the

entitled are broadcasted and mocked ubiquitously. The fundamental fault in the inflated ego is that it thinks that it will remain supreme purely because of its talents, fame, or fortune. There always comes that fateful day when the ego realizes that its easily replaced.

Those with an unhealthy ego believe they deserve a certain standard of living and respect, whether earned or not. This is especially true of those who became famous for reasons other than their personal or professional achievement. The inflated self-important ego tends to view every situation, dispute, or thwarted expectation as a personal affront that needs to be defended. A threatened the out-of-control ego will feel victimized, unrealistically filtering the importance or intent of certain events involving or comments about them. Deep down, that ego feels like a fake about to be discovered for its perpetrated fraud upon society.

To keep your ego strong and capable, keep connected to the familiar of your life before your stardom. At the age of twenty, popular singer Selena Gomez revealed she still drives the same car she's driven since the age of sixteen and continues to live with her parents. The on-again-off-again Justin Bieber girlfriend is happiest when performing.

Actress and model Brooke Shields made the transition from a child to an adult star without a major meltdown. Even with her exposure to the wild parties at the New York nightclub Studio 54, Andy Warhol and his ever-present Superstars were very protective of Shields and the sweet naiveté of a normal childhood. Academy Award winning actress Jennifer Lawrence appreciates her opportunity. Raised to value and respect money, she still balks at hotel mini-bar charges of six bucks for a candy bar. Lawrence said she was raised by a family who would never let her turn into a diva or, in her words, an *a--hole*.

How to Cope When Everybody Wants You

So many people around me would say they cared for the wrong reasons. A lot of people were pulling from me, taking from me and not giving.
                                                — *Lindsay Lohan*

Everyone wants a piece of you. The media, the paparazzi, your fans, onlookers and rubberneckers, the people who surround you, your entourage, your family, the professionals you hired or are hired by your agent or your company (whose job it is to make you popular or keep the ratings high), all stand to gain through their relationship with you. Everyone seems to have an angle. Some long to be you. Others want what you have. Still others want admiration, validation, acknowledgement, or power. Survival as an in-demand high-profile person depends on understanding and setting good boundaries and sticking with them and in knowing how to act in public to maintain your image.

Managing fame and celebrity is a tricky business. It's hard to keep your boundaries intact. You have to deal with the same people every day, and you might not like all of them. Your home is a tour bus, hotels, airplanes, or a limo. You're away from for the people you care about for long periods of time. You get demands from everyone and start to feel you are not in control of the decisions about your life, and you feel you are losing control.

You answer the same inane interview questions six times a day. You don't get much sleep because of the shooting or touring schedule. You don't eat right or exercise regularly because you are on the road or on location. The list is endless, and you feel 24/7 pressure and stress. Ignoring the situation or covering it up through misguided coping behavior just makes it worse.

Find and use healthy stress outlets and stress management techniques. Make time to recharge and recoup. Take the time to rest, eat, exercise, practice your spirituality, and spend time with what gives you energy. Staying connected to those who love you for who you are and who don't give a damn about your fame will help you stay face each day feeling grounded and supported.

Keep your private life as simple and uncomplicated as possible. Take a time out when you need it. Getting some simple peace and quiet can alleviate some of its impact on your quality of life. A time out can be as simple as a request for 10 minutes of alone time so you can breathe and collect your thoughts. Learning how to calmly and rationally express your needs in a way they can be heard, understood, and acknowledged will mitigate much of the pressure.

Do what you can to learn from others mistakes. You've witnessed dozens who've succumbed to the relentless impositions and let fame get the upper hand. Acknowledge the reality of your situation, with a focus on its benefits rather than its hindrances.

Enjoy the freedom that fame brings instead of being stifled by it. Thrive on fame instead of merely coping with it. Maintain a fierce guardianship over your truth instead of your conditioned programming.

If you're in a reality television show, you may be pressured upon to act as a cartoon version of your natural nature, as if that exaggerated character is the real you. If you're a contestant vying for a talent or any other type of competitive title, you're under an enormous amount of pressure and stress to be the best you can be under the watchful critical eyes of the viewing audience. A lot is riding on whether or not you win the holy grail of being named the best of the best. Your immediate career prospects and future financial potential may be at stake.

While winners don't necessarily take all, they walk away with exceptional opportunities. Keeping closely connected to those who support you, no matter what, and those who encourage your greatness will help you focused and fully prepared to face the challenge. Ultimately, though, only you can rigorously challenge your inner status quo if it distracts you from actualizing a winning performance.

Embrace a Healthy Self-Esteem

Once you start living in that fame world you can start believing it, and it's just so bad for you. That's not the real world. All of this one day will go away no matter who you are, and I need to be OK with who I am as myself and this doesn't make or break me. This is wonderful and I love this ride but I'm also so blessed without it as well.

– Khloe Kardashian

While cherished, published, and admired, many celebrities harbor low self-esteem or admit to self-confidence problems. Are those who reach the pinnacle of fame insecure because they're famous or are they famous because they're insecure? In a 2012 interview with *Harper's Bazaar*, Demi Moore talked about her split with Ashton Kutcher and subsequent rehab. She said that what scared her was that there was something fundamentally wrong with her. She feared that she would ultimately find out at the end of her life that she's really not loveable, not worthy of being loved, and wasn't wanted here in the first place.

Your worst critic is the nattering nabob of negativity within you. She will nag and belittle you because she wants you to stay small so you'll be safe. That's all she knows how to do. The trouble is, she's very misguided in what will keep you safe.

When you were a little child, you developed this inner voice to guide you and keep you from danger. Serving as the guardian of your feelings and your ability to stay embraced by those who took care of you, she developed a book of life rules for you to follow. Some common rules are:

- I'm not good, smart, worthy, loveable, respected, valued, or whatever *enough*.
- I'll never amount to anything.
- It's better to give than to receive.
- Better safe than sorry.
- You have to claw your way to the top.

The set of life commandments you created as a child became your operating system. It served it purpose. It got you out of childhood alive and to a certain level of success. You continue to view the circumstances and events of your life through this filter. Yet like all computer programs, the code gets outdated with time. The areas of life in which you struggle are indicators where its time for an internal update.

When you're unconsciously directed by a message from childhood that doesn't work for you, you're at cross-purposes. You unknowingly work against yourself. For example, if you feel you're not *whatever* enough, you'll seek out proof of this claim. You'll view your career opportunities and personal relationships from this perspective to show evidence of your lack. You'll have a hard time dealing objectively with the criticism, rejection, and scrutiny that come with the territory of your chosen pursuit.

Or if you believe deep down inside that it's better to give then to receive then you'll beat yourself up for being a horrible person for having received so much. Pretty soon, you'll work your way out of having what you once acquired. You could become the kind of person who's never happy or satisfied because the more you receive, the more you feel pressured to give. It's exhausting to spend your days fighting an internal battle that gets you deeper and deeper into a rut.

Keep the rules that work for you. These are the inner messages that make you feel good and empowered. Identify and reframe the rules that don't work for you. Reach for another perspective when the one you have diminishes rather than uplifts how you feel. This practice isn't about eliminating negative beliefs. Chances are slim you'll get rid of all of them. I don't know anyone who has. The thing to do is to recognize the babblecrap you tell yourself without automatically acting upon those thoughts. Remember, there's no such thing as "peace of mind," for it is the mind that disrupts the peace.

The thing is, you can't change anything you can't see. Embrace a better perspective and take steps in that direction. Pay attention to how you feel, for your emotions are indicators of whether or not you're in flow or embroiled in an inner duel. A client of mine has chosen to say to herself *Hear ya, not gonna be ya*, when prompted by a tired old belief that has long lost its value. This isn't about attaching yourself to any cheesy positive thinking mumbo jumbo. You overcome negative self-talk by getting out there and being productive. Stop whining or complaining and just get something done. Remember how accomplishment feels? That's the vibe that shifts your world. The resistant and reluctant inner voice is always calmed by a creative flow.

I don't believe anyone was born a mistake. Everyone is worthy of love. Everyone is born with the potential to make a meaningful contribution. If you hold yourself back because you feel less than somehow, you rob the world of the gift you were brought into this world to give. I often tell my clients their greatness is at the tip of their nose. That's why they can't see it. All I do is hold up a mirror and hold them lovingly accountable to their fullest potential. It's what they, and

I, are here to do. It's what you're here to do.

You owe it to yourself to embrace the whole of you. Every bit of you has meaning and purpose. What you may see as flaws are either beauty unacknowledged or opportunities to learn and grow. They have tremendous value. Instead of shunning or shaming any piece of you, bring out its brilliance. Be a shining star from the inside out.

The Impostor Syndrome

As a young man, I prayed for success. Now I just pray to be worthy of it.

– Brendan Fraser

Imagine the feeling that everything you have accomplished is little more than luck, happenstance, and a matter of being in the right place at the right time and doing exactly the right thing.

Roll some cosmic dice anyone?

The Impostor Syndrome among celebrities is a condition that is the subject of an increasing number of studies. In short, impostor syndrome is a belief that everything the person has accomplished is a result of random chance and luck rather than merit. The person's actual abilities have nothing to do with the success.

Diablo Cody is the writer behind *Juno, Jennifer's Body, Young Adult*, and the hit show, *The United States of Tara*. She is one famous and highly successful woman who suffers from the all-too-common belief that she isn't as good as people think she is. Yet, despite the nagging doubts that assail her, she pushes through. And that's the key. Cody moves forward anyway, even though she may fear that it's only a matter of time before she's "found out" to be "less than" her perceived value.

Columnist Amelia McDonell-Parry pointed to an interview Cody gave to Movies.com about the condition to announce she too suffers: "Even though I know I work hard, I'm not always sure that I'm worthy of the success that I've had. In my lower self-esteem moments, I don't believe I'm capable of achieving more than I already have. I certainly compare myself to other women in my peer group who, in my mind, have done 'more'—authors I admire like Rachel Shukert, for example or comedians/writers like Mindy Kaling—and feel like a hack in comparison."

While some self-doubts are to be expected in anyone, those who suffer from Impostor Syndrome have doubts that reach far deeper. Michelle Pfeiffer once said, "I still think people will find out that I'm really not very talented. I'm really not very good. It's all been a big sham."

Actor Tom Hanks was asked how he felt about doubting oneself while playing the role of a journalist in Nora Ephron's last work *Lucky Guy*. He said about the play, "Look, the title is *Lucky Guy*. It's about somebody who is almost good enough to deserve what he achieves. And I understand that. I see some other actor's work and I think I'll never get there. I wish I could."

While there are many stories of people with Impostor Syndrome who have successful careers based on their achievement, no formal studies have been done those who may have let this condition take such control of their life that they don't even try. Susan Pinker wrote *The Sexual Paradox: Troubled Boys, Gifted Girls and the Real Difference Between the Sexes* and devoted an entire chapter to Impostor Syndrome. In the book, she says this is strictly limited to successful women. Satoshi Kanazawa, an evolutionary psychologist, is also taking a look at the matter. He notes Impostor Syndrome appears to be far more common in women, making it a gender based matter. Referring to research on a somewhat related matter called "causal attribution," Dr. Kanazawa said evidence points to a marked difference in men and women there. While the phenomenon may only affect women in the general corporate environment, I believe men as well as women experience the Impostor Syndrome within the high-profile community.

Celebrities are often seen as heroes, as role models, representing desired qualities or having the fame and acceptance many want to achieve for themselves. This may be why I see evidence of the Impostor Syndrome in some of the high-profile women and men I have the privilege to mentor. Perhaps the more seemingly unrealistic the praise, the more likely it is to affect both genders.

To rise above the Impostor Syndrome, it is essential to rigorously challenge your inner *status quo*. Worthiness isn't dependent upon perfection. Recognize when you feel like an impostor. Sit with that feeling for a moment and let that energy dissipate.

Remember that as long as we have breath within us we have room to grow, learn, and become better. Feeling like an impostor is just your soul reminding you that you have much more within you to express before you reach your highest potential.

Know this: When your ego has run amok, it will steal away your ability to make good choices in your personal and professional life. It's only a matter of time before it will slam you into a wall as you engage in risky or provocative behavior. The lights will be turned out on your bright future. A healthy dose of humility and humanity will restore you to the driver's seat of your situation. A realistic sense of self will keep you grounded and connected to the heartbeat of humanity.

Keep Your Cool

Eventually stardom is going to go away from me. It goes away from everybody and all you have in the end is to be able to look back and like the choices you made.

– Matt Damon

If you find yourself flippin' around like a rattlesnake on PCP from one crisis to the next you're on the habitrail of disaster. Albert Einstein defined insanity as doing the same thing over and over again expecting different results. The same goes for your behavior. The public has little or no compassion for your problems. When you're emotionally wrapped up in your own hype, you can easily get triggered. The simplest little thing can send you reeling into the hot mess of crazytown. Tantrums worthy of a two-year-old are common because a two-year-old, also, has an out of control ego. The difference is: you're a grown up. You know better.

Supermodel Naomi Campbell hit her housekeeper on the head with a phone over an incident regarding a pair of jeans. Campbell was arraigned on second-degree assault charges largely because the attack upon the housekeeper caused lacerations that required stitches to heal properly. In an earlier incident, Campbell pleaded guilty in Toronto to an assault charge for beating an assistant during the making of a 1998 movie.

Amanda Bynes' self-inflicted problems and public wackiness is tragic. She's had multiple hit-and-run charges after a DUI arrest in 2012. Tirades, outrageous tweets, and bizarre accusations followed in a desperate attempt to make the problems go away. She's certainly not the first former child star to destruct under grown-up pressures.

Lindsay Lohan's transition to responsible adult life derailed. As I write this, the world is still waiting for this incredibly talented actress to get her act together. Britney Spears, Miley Cyrus, and Justin Beiber are among contemporary youths who have experienced difficulties growing up in the fishbowl of public awareness. Comedian Jeff Garlin was booked on felony vandalism when he allegedly smashed a car's window during a fight over a parking space. Your best bet is to curb your enthusiasm when it comes to emotional outbursts. Life is easier when you use your words, not your fists, to communicate. When life comes along and knocks you on your ass, it's humbling. It's up to you whether you embrace and retain that humility or tell it to get bent and go back to your self-centric ways. There is profound opportunity in the dark night of the soul. Reach deeply beneath your surface to find the soul in need.

If you've created a predicament that can be catastrophic to your career, engage an expert crisis management company immediately to get ahead of the news cycle. If you don't lead the telling of your story, someone else will, and you won't like the tale told. Whether you're a high-profile personality in trouble or a head of a scandal-plagued organization, get crackerjack specialists to navigate your controversy to the best possible result. Quick action will enable your consultant to strike fast by getting the facts, assess the situation, and establish a strategy in a matter of minutes. Rather than worry about getting the last word, have someone craft your first word on the matter to set the tone for the coverage that follows. Strictly heed the advice of these damage control masters. They know what they're doing.

While big problems require big guns to handle the situation, small problems that become big problems are often unnecessary. You have the power to avoid them completely. One of the most ridiculous hissy fits may have been by rock icon Eddie Van Halen when he discovered brown chocolate M&M's in the band's candy dish. He had a clause in his contract strictly detailing all food, drink, and other paraphernalia that was to be provided in the dressing room. The offending candies were a definite no-no and Van Halen freaked, doing about $85,000 worth of damage to a backstage room. The lapse in sound judgment received more press than the concert itself.

Stories like these have long legs and can last in perpetuity. Whenever one of your colleagues has an over-the-top snit-fit, their misguided behavior will be rebroadcast again and again. The outburst just isn't worth it. Fame and dealing with celebrity is stressful. That's all the more reason to keep alert and guarded under pressure.

The constant attention that comes with fame inflates some celebrities' egos. For others though, the effect is the reverse: it makes them so aware of their shortcomings that they may be driven to self-destruction. If you screw up, own it. Follow David Letterman's example when he was forced by a blackmailer to make an adulterous affair public. Show up. Own up. Shut up. Address gossip in a timely fashion. If there's truth in the story—if you've committed a mistake of some sort—admit it. It requires courage to acknowledge your mistakes. It's foolish to let the media have the satisfaction by reacting turning an acorn of an incident into a mighty oak tree with deep roots. Doing so only adds insult to injury, allowing the media to sell more magazines, get more viewers, and please more advertisers—at your expense.

Don't try to explain away your fall from grace. Sounding like a soap opera queen with the drama of being defensive, self-pitying, and paranoid will not deliver the results you want. Having a cavalier attitude or blaming some baddie "out there" out to get you over jealously of your success will undermine your success. Even if you've been "done wrong," with personal outrage, less is more. Keep your ego in check.

If you slip up, apologize. With sincerity. Have the courage to reveal your vulnerability and your fans will admire you for it. It gives them hope in the possibility that they, too, will be okay if their vulnerabilities are exposed. You will live to enjoy your fame instead of falling from grace and fading away.

Ignore the people who gossip about you behind your back. They're right where they belong: behind you. It's very easy to get carried away and react to stories in a knee-jerk fashion. It requires a maturity that comes with experience to not take everything at face value and see the intricacies beneath the surface. Positive action is the best way to put your mistakes in the past.

Integral to owning and learning from your mistakes is getting real about the situation you've created through your misguided choices. Know the terrain you created. Instead of glossing over the mess you've made or seeing your circumstance as worse that it really is, get a proper perspective. Know what you're up against. Seek to understand how the issue impacts everyone involved. Know the facts and how, specifically, the outcome evolved. Without judgment, discern the role you played in the story. Beating yourself up is a waste of time and energy. Channel those resources to creating newer and better outcomes going forward.

If you've really done it, committed a heinous error or led yourself down a treacherous path, making a mountain out of a molehill of a problem call in an expert crisis manager, and for the love-of-all-you-hold-sacred, follow his or her advice without exception. You'll pay heavily for such expert consultation. Get a solid return on your investment by being a model client.

Drug and Alcohol Addiction

*It's hard to get out of the barrel. It's slippery around
the edges and people are happy to see you fall back in.*
– Robert Downey, Jr.

Unfortunately, fame and fortune doesn't guarantee a free pass on inner angst. The paradox is that it can generate or enrich the agony that lurks within. Addiction leads the list of celebrity problems. Living life openly vulnerable in the gilded cage is stressful. It takes a strong conviction and sense of purpose to cope. The pleasure found in finally arriving can quickly turn into a desperate quest to escape the pressure.

To numb the pain, illegal or pharmaceutical drugs and/or alcohol are readily available solutions. The problem is, you can't isolate which emotion to numb. When you numb pain, you also numb joy. Joyless, you reach for your drug of choice as a quick fix. The high quickly wears off, and you're out looking for your next hit. Continuing to use a substance—even when it causes major life problems—defines addiction. The disease strikes without regard for status, wealth, gender, or age. The mutual attraction of celebrities and addiction can become fatal.

In the public eye, the desire to escape the constant scrutiny and the lack of privacy can lead you to chemicals simply to escape. You have more access to drugs because you have the financial resources and a network of people seeking our attention and approval. Underneath it all though, you are still human with the same problems and weaknesses as everyone else.

Living in a fishbowl, with your crazy schedule and the unreasonable demands you face, only intensifies the power of your inner demons. Your managers, agents, handlers, and entourage, all enable you to continue using by working hard to keep you safe from the consequences of your actions. It is their job to "spin" things into positive press and attention to keep your brand going strong even if you're coming undone.

Perhaps your fame balances on how you look or how well you perform. As a star, you may feel the need to be in "star mode" all the time. Not only is it an exhausting way to live, being "on" all the time never gives you time to replenish in a meaningful way. Addiction among the high-profile elite isn't limited to celebrities. Richard's high-end clientele include a large percentage of powerful executives who cling to prescription drugs or alcohol as a security blanket. The more demanding the job the more pharmaceuticals and booze is misguidedly used to work longer, harder, better, clearer, or more creatively. The drug of choice works initially, and then it lets you down, piling problems on top of more problems with which to deal. The pressure is intense. What starts out as a lark soon escalates into a nightmare with lots of trouble and heartache. This is why pharmaceuticals and other misguided coping mechanisms become an attractive and easy solution for a quick fix or escape.

Eating disorders also manifest under the pressure of the critical public eye. Princess Diana suffered from bulimia. Singer Karen Carpenter died from complications caused by anorexia. There has been speculation about eating disorders surrounding Calista Flockhart, Victoria Beckham, Christina Ricci, Portia De Rossi, Sharon Osbourne, Ashlee Simpson, Ginger Spice Geri Halliwell, Mary Kate Olsen, and many others. Anorexia really isn't about food or weight. It's a mistaken response to fulfill the emotional needs that come from depression, loneliness, insecurity, pressure to be perfect, or a feeling of not being in control. When you spend most of your time thinking about food, dieting, and weight loss, you don't have to face the other problems in your life or face complicated emotions that cry for help. In order to survive—or at least have the strength and energy to live a quality life—at some point that cry needs to be answered, preferably with professional and immediate support.

Addiction doesn't go away, and it has no cure. It is said: once an addict, always an addict. With treatment and lifestyle changes, you can be a thriving addict in recovery as opposed to a struggling addict in a never-ending downward spiral. Addictions trigger the reward centers in our brains, releasing dopamine. This is a "reward" chemical that causes the brain damage with repeated abuse. An unhealthy addiction damages your body, mind, and spirit. It derails the relationship you have with your close and wider support network. The wreckage it can cause your career, and by extension your value as a celebrity, is overwhelming. As an addiction progresses, emotions become a perfectly stirred cocktail of anger and confusion. The world witnesses a very public celebrity meltdown as the disease claims the mental and physical health of yet another one among you.

Celebrities behaving badly are a mainstay of the entertainment industry. Your profession has a well-earned reputation for hard-partying and wild lifestyle. Many who are new to fame have idolized this reputation for years. Some circles celebrate and encourage addictive behaviors. Rarely is the word "no" heard when you demand something from your team because "no" tends to be a surefire ticket to the unemployment line. It's important to remember the Upton Sinclair line: "It is difficult to get a man to understand something, when his salary depends on his not understanding it." Your entourage *will not tell you something is wrong* as long as pleasing you is their main job. Their job depends on enabling your addiction—at least in the short run.

Raging addiction is painful to experience and painful to watch. The toll of celebrity addiction is heavy with the loss of talents such as Amy Winehouse, John Belushi, Jean-Michel Basquiat, Elvis Presley, Keith Moon, Lenny Bruce, Chris Farley, Judy Garland, Jimmi Hendrix, Janis Joplin, Whitney Houston, Heath Ledger, River Phoenix, Ike Turner, Sid Vicious, Marilyn Monroe, and many more. Others, such as Lindsay Lohan, Daniel Baldwin, Jeff Conaway, Tatum O'Neal, Artie Lange, Philip Seymour Hoffman, Gerard Bulter, Charlie Sheen, Gary Busey, Mackenzie Philips, Tom Sizemore, Dennis Rodman, Leif Garrett, Eric Roberts, Courtney Love, Sean Young, and countless others enter rehab—sometimes again and again—struggling to kick the habit.

The good news is many have succeeded in their determination to remain solidly in recovery. Robert Downey Jr., Slash (of Guns and Roses), Eric Clapton, Eminem, Steven Tyler, Drew Barrymore, Elton John, Martin Sheen, Jamie Lee Curtis, Kelly Osbourne, Robin Williams, Nicole Richie are just a few fine examples. Oh, let's not forget Oprah—yes, Oprah. She admitted on her show about her use and, perhaps abuse, of crack cocaine when she was in her 20s, and after that she built a media empire. Addiction can be overcome, and there is a life afterwards.

Acknowledging an addiction can be frightening. It seems as if the whole world is crumbling beneath you. The irony is that what feels like an unraveling is often a coming together. You can get help. There are many excellent rehab facilities that cater to the unique privacy needs of the high-profiled. The list includes Promises Treatment Center, Cirque Lodge, Passages Rehab Facility, The Meadows, The Betty Ford Clinic, Destination Hope, Prive Swiss, Wonderland, Crossroads, and Cliffside Malibu.

If you end up in rehab and make it through the program, the celebrity lifestyle is still right in front of you, waiting for your return. Staying away can be nearly impossible. Relapsing, thanks to drugs offered to you daily, may be the next step. So be ready: successful recovery from addiction might require you to avoid the lifestyle, the people, and the triggers that led you to abuse substances in the first place.

That sounds almost like giving up being famous to some people. Many of your friends struggle with maintaining their sobriety simply because they will not or cannot give up the perks of fame. Instead of focusing on the availability of material excesses, work on developing stronger inner resources. Deal with pride and vanity as obstacles on the road to recovery, while building a generous, giving environment that fosters the mental and social health of everyone around you, including yourself.

Famous addicts are the same as everyone else. Addiction is a disease. If you want to recover, you must aim high and use your resources to give yourself time and opportunity to let your brain and body heal. Be realistic about what you can handle and what you need to do to stay sane and healthy. After all, your fame depends on your body, your looks, and your brains. You cannot afford to damage the source of the gifts you've received. Addict or not, cultivate your self-awareness, your humility, and your awareness of your true self to avoid chemical entanglements from which you might never emerge.

Those who are dedicated to their recovery go through a period of redemption where a return to positive celebrity status is initiated through a public admission of their struggle and a request for public absolution. The acceptance of the redemption request isn't guaranteed. One may never regain the level of eminence once realized, but the public loves a redemption story almost as much as they love to see a celebrity fail. You'll get one more chance. Make the most of it.

A Visit to Cliffside Malibu

If you're going through hell I suggest you come back learning something.

– Drew Barrymore

Richard Taite, a former addict, is the founder and spirit of Cliffside Malibu. I drove up the windy hilly road to visit with him and talk about his perspective on addiction, treatment, and the unique needs of the wealthy and famous clientele.

I visited with Richard Taite, Founder and CEO, to see what a first-class treatment center truly brought to troubled celebrities and discover some of what he's learned from his experiences. From the moment my bare feet touched the earth of Cliffside Malibu, a luxury treatment facility, I knew I was in the garden of centered souls. Unencumbered by my ridiculous choice of stilettos, I was very curious to connect with the man who planted the seeds, provided the nourishment, and brought in the sunlight that inspired such abundant growth.

I realized Cliffside Malibu was a reflection of the person Richard had become. It is a kind, gentle, quiet place that births an environment for a profound connection with the human spirit within all those who arrive to help them find what they seek. Richard serves as the compassionate and devoted parent welcoming and honoring his 'family' into a home he created for them. With genuine esteem for all who arrive, he is there to serve the highest good of all who come through the door.

Richard's story, his journey home to who he was born to become, how he makes a difference in the world and in the lives of who he serves, is a story I am privileged to share with you.

Inevitably there is a defining moment or two within each person's life that sets the course that will reach the final destination. We all know that, for each of us, death is the ultimate outcome. Life's meaning is discovered in your purposeful journey—not your bling. How we feel as we reflect upon the life we've lived and the legacy we leave is largely a result of the choices we made in the defining moments that presented themselves years, even decades, before.

Richard had a few such moments. He had a difficult childhood that included physical abuse and unhealthy parental influences. He was introduced to illegal drugs as a 12-year-old boy when 'time with Dad' alternately meant smoking pot and being beaten with a cane.

In 1998, he was a young adult in the throws of a very destructive cocaine addiction that left him over $300,000 in debt, without a job, no family relationships, and no self-esteem. He was kiting checks to support his addiction. The bank president caught the fraudulent checks and informed Richard that if he didn't stop immediately, he would be reported to the authorities. This was a defining moment, even if Richard didn't realize it at the time. This 'Godshot' prevented him from what could have been the first in a series of prison sentences.

As I listened to Richard tell his story, I couldn't help but wonder how much of his choice to turn to drugs as a coping mechanism upon entering adulthood was influenced by his childhood growing up with his Dad. Did what it is to "be a man" equal doing drugs and beating himself up in this misguided young child's mind?

Richard had one friend other than the banker. Thin, facing homelessness, and with only $50 to his name, Richard went to that friend and asked for $1000 in a last ditch effort to survive.

As his friend was ready to hand over the thousand dollars, Richard had his first recognized defining moment. He had the presence of mind to know what he did with that $1000 would chart the course of his life from that moment on. He knew if he took the money in cash, he would find an excuse to spend it on more drugs to soothe his inner pain. He'd be left worse off because he would then have lost his only friend.

In that moment, that moment of clarity, Richard had his friend make the check out to a sober living facility, giving Richard no choice but to check himself in. He had nowhere else to go. He got sober.

While the story has a happy ending, Richard had a journey to travel before he finally got to the place he is today. He was clean, doing well financially, yet still not committed to a healthy life. The emotional triggers that drove him to drugs still lay active within him. He continued to have an on-again, off-again relationship with his addiction. But at least he was sober enough of the time to tap back into the inner voice of clarity that guided him so well during his first defining moment.

In the next moment, Richard realized that the problem he had with drugs wasn't because of external factors in his life. The problem was himself—and how he showed up to his life. Finally, Richard was willing to take responsibility for the life he created and what he would create from that moment forward.

Until someone is willing to be the cause instead of the effect of his life circumstance, meaningful change is impossible. With a good therapist, Richard was able to uncover the reasons and issues behind his addiction. He was able to transform them into what would feed his soul instead of diminish it. With a renewed sense of self and a healthier relationship with what mattered most in life, Richard achieved sobriety on March 23, 2003.

Fast forward to a year later. Richard bought a sprawling property high on a hill in Malibu with a spectacular ocean view. He lived alone in this spacious house and enjoyed its serenity. One night, he had an epiphany. The purpose of the house wasn't meant to be a residence. It had a higher purpose. He had a higher purpose.

The experiences in Richard's life—good and bad—meant something. Having gone through the life he led, he knows what it means to feel empty desperately looking for a quick fix to fill the hole within. His journey to sobriety and beyond taught him what it means to feel whole and what it takes to achieve it. He knows with certainty that self-esteem, a sustained sense of wellbeing, and peace of mind doesn't come packaged in a pill, bottle, co-dependent relationship, or symbol of material wealth. Fulfillment is an inside job.

These experiences gave him something uniquely of value in knowledge and wisdom that he could share with the world. With that awareness, Richard bought and moved into a nearby home and transformed what was his private home into what is now Cliffside Malibu. He kept the integrity of its privacy, quiet elegance, and peaceful, nurturing 'vibe'. It was designed and staffed to accommodate client guests in a way that showed respect for their challenge and a profound acceptance for who they are as a whole human being— mind, body, and soul.

Addictions come in many forms: drugs, alcohol, sex, gambling, food, or any number of other misguided behaviors to calm emotional and physical pain. As a former addict, Richard knows on a visceral level how his clients feel when they arrive.

The luxury setting and amenities aren't there to impress. They have a very specific healing purpose. As a former addict, he's mindful that an addict is always looking for an excuse to quit a program that will take him (or her) back to sobriety, away from what he craves most. The setting high on the hill in Malibu with a spectacular ocean view, a staff of excellence, luxury amenities, and beautiful surroundings makes it hard for a client to find an excuse to say "Screw this place, I'm out of here," and leave before completing the program.

Richard believes the top two paramount issues that create drug-addicted behavior are trauma and not getting needs met as a child. The desire to self-medicate to overcome physical and/or emotional pain of trauma is relatively easy to understand. The harder issue, according to Richard, is unmet childhood needs. This isn't about food, clothing, and lots of toys. It's an emotional void.

For example, if parents or caregivers didn't make a child feel important, then that child may think that he isn't important enough to be paid any attention. She may feel unlovable, like a piece of garbage or "not enough." As with physical trauma, medication seems to be the obvious answer to this chronic form of trauma. This is why Richard takes a personal interest in each person's journey back to health, as if he was the parent, the Father he wished he once had—one who enriched and empowered his children.

The importance that comes with fame does little to mitigate such deep-rooted trauma. Conversely, it can exacerbate the exasperation. There isn't enough positive attention in the world to heal the childhood wound if the child within still feels unworthy.

Richard's mission and purpose in life is predicated on real, long-lasting, meaningful change within those who come through his door.

Why? Because Richard knows the powerful difference such a human connection makes in the life and journey of all human beings. Today, Richard gets high daily on his sense of purpose, as a man, husband, and father. His emptiness is now filled with love, humility, respect for fellow mankind, his esteem for those he serves, and a profound appreciation of the real abundance life has to offer—reflected in the eyes, smile, and heart of his daughter.

Reconnected with his innate goodness, compassion, dedication to his purpose and personal spirituality, Richard is home.

Family and Friends

Every day I work at not taking this fame thing seriously. Fortunately, I have a great group of friends who help me do this.

– Bruce Willis

As you transition your life as a private citizen to a famous personality, maintain your connection with your family and close friends. The sudden and copious changes you experience compound the stress of new responsibility. Retaining the familiar around you will help you adjust and keep your feet on the ground.

Hollywood marriages are notoriously short. The media documents a typically skewed play-by-play essay on troubled marriages. Lasting marriages get little coverage, except when featured in articles about long standing relationships among the rich and famous. While each relationship is unique, many unions fall apart because of unrealistic expectations, the impulsive nature of the relationship itself, the reason for the marriage in the first place (celebrity stunt, career boost, etc.), or the effects of the celebrity culture with high rates of infidelity, egotism, unrealistic dreams, and immaturity.

Celebrity marriages that have gone the distance include Tom Hanks and Rita Wilson, Sara Jessica Parker and Matthew Broderick, Michael J. Fox and Tracy Pollan, John Travolta and Kelly Preston, Bono and Ali Hewson, Jamie Lee Curtis and Christopher Guest, Kevin Bacon and Kyra Sedgwick, Antonio Banderas and Melanie Griffith, Denzel and Pauletta Washington, Warren Beatty and Annette Benning, Michelle Pfeiffer and David E. Kelley, and David Bowie and supermodel Iman. Secrets to their success include meaningful conversation, the ability to make each other laugh, mutual trust and respect, honesty, similar backgrounds, shared values, integrity, and never taking one another for granted. It takes a solid investment of time, energy, and commitment to an intimate relationship to keep it fresh and interesting over a span of many decades.

Successful writer and actor Ben Watkins looks to his wife to keep him grounded. They married when he was still struggling. She helps keep him grounded reminding him who he is, who they are as a couple and family, where they come from, and what they care about. They grow together as Watkins becomes more and more successful.

With that success comes greater public awareness. Being recognized by the public can result in a raid on your personal space. Your family is also invaded. If you neglect to step outside of notoriety to communicate with those closest to you, resentment will breed. Talk about the situation and what can be done about it. Discuss the impact your career has upon the family, individually and as a whole.

Your working hours may be ridiculous. The time you have to spend away from home might be absurdly excessive. Tell your family that you're availability to them will be reduced. Understanding it and dealing with the issues of your absence is another issue you have to deal with to keep your family whole. Ignoring it or wishing the problem would go away isn't a solution.

Distance yourself from emotionally charged situations. Sit down with your family; as a group, determine whether or not the sacrifice is worth it. If it is, decide as a family to embrace the absence as part of the process to achieve the bigger vision. If it isn't, be prepared to change the course.

Everyone will make compromises. Hard decisions must be made

together. If you value your family, keep family as a priority. Redefine career expectations—if you have to—because a career is transitory. Even if it reaches the loftiest of expectations, it will still never replace having a strong family behind you.

Remember, the people who matter to you most are not just your fans. Of course, your fans love you, but they can also hate you if you do not live up to their (often unrealistic) expectations. Unlike your close friends and family, who will be there for you now and later when all this is over, fans will laud you, lower you, and leave you for the next bright shining star without a second thought.

Keep your family and friend relationships apart from that of your staff and followers. Do not make the mistake of clubbing them together with the hordes of people who wish to examine your life as if you were living in a fish bowl. Unlike the masses that only know you as a persona, the people closest to you know and love you for who you really are. Like-minded or not, these are the people that make your heart sing.

If you've kept childhood friends as you grew into adulthood, keep them near and dear as you grow into stardom. There's nothing that keeps you grounded in reality more than someone who knows the difference between the hyped persona and the person you see in the mirror every day. If your ego starts sucking all the air out of the room, a true friend will call you on it, bursting its expanse. You may not like what you hear, yet its better to be cautioned privately by someone who truly cares about you than remain blind to a forthcoming eruption.

Friends and family members quickly turn into "frenemies" when audacity dukes it out. Keep disagreements with your BFF's and family issues out of the public conversation. Refrain from commenting on your relationships with those you love unless you have something positive to say. The boomerang of karmic fate will get you if you dole out dish.

The bottom line is, shop girls and people you pay aren't your friends. Your friends are those who are there for you, not your fame. They are the people you trust to have your best interests at heart. They are the people you will be there for as well. If you're going to have an entourage, model it after the "based on a real story" television show, *Entourage*. The main character, Vince, formed friendships with his faithful friends long before he became rich and famous. He employed his friends as "staff" because they were talented, and they needed the association in order to get started on their own rise to stardom. Essentially, Vince bails them out of their challenging circumstances, and in turn, they bail him out of his struggles as they occur. You want to surround yourself with people you trust who support and help you as you would do for them. Otherwise, the price of a steady group of loyal supporters is dear and, too often, you don't get the trust you paid for.

For a busy in-demand person, it's helpful to have people who know you available to serve your needs, whether it's for a casual purchase or for day-to-day staffed support. Assuming that these people are friends at the ready to serve you at their fullest capacity without compensation of any kind is misguided. Genuine affinity and sincerity (in a culture that builds relationships on a foundation of personal agendas and selfish gain) exists—but it isn't easy to find.

What are the 6 main qualities in a true friend?

    1. You can entrust your deepest darkest secrets without

worrying that your confidences will end up on TMZ, Page 6, or become the latest topic of conversation to hit the social grapevine.

2. When life throws you a curveball, a friends first question to you is: "What do you need?"—and he makes sure you get it (or at least he genuinely tries).

3. A friend champions your dream with enthusiasm, even if she doesn't agree with or understand it, and tries to help you avoid some of the pitfalls on the way.

4. He will pick you up at two a.m. when your car breaks down twenty miles out of town and without complaint. (Well, not serious complaint, anyway.)

5. She honors the integrity of your friendship in front of others who aren't as friendly.

6. Values herself enough to invest most of her "friend" time and energy with only the friends who would do the same for her.

A true friend consistently expresses these qualities without compensation, without keeping score, and without requiring *quid pro quo*. But remember, a true friendship is when there is a natural free exchange of quality time, interest, and honest communication. You can't get that kind of respect and dedication through a placement service. Friendships aren't just one-way, either.

When friends or family members are involved in the business of your celebrity, make sure to keep clear boundaries between your business and personal relationship. If desired results aren't produced, treat them as you would any other employee, even if it means gathering up your courage as you politely show them the door. You can go out together for tea and cupcakes later on. Again, the TV show *Entourage* shows how Vince (the celebrity) and his friends (first) Eric and Turtle are grow as employees, championed when merited or limited when too reliant on Vincent's celebrity, and he happily lets them find their own path when they've moved later as entrepreneurs.

How to Handle a Break-Up

Pour yourself a drink, put on some lipstick, and pull yourself together.

– Elizabeth Taylor

Breakups permeate the celebrity community.

As a celebrity with means, it's a lot easier in some ways to go through a break-up. It's likely you have financial assets of your own and don't have to consider the money side of the situation. You can hire a good lawyer and take care of your own living expenses. While there are no guarantees, the fear of never meeting a future life partner is mitigated by the many people you meet through work and your public appearances.

In fact, infidelity is a common catalyst for the dissolution of a relationship. There is heightened temptation when you're a magnet for fame by association. Celebrity careers are demanding, with a lot of time often spent away from home, working with and meeting others who have their own magnetic attraction.

Know that if you or your partner cheats, the public will know. Stories of cheating scandals, whether true or not, run rampant in the tabloids. Once the media picks upon a possible affair, you will be asked to comment. Consider the potential long-term impact of your remarks as well as how they can affect other people, especially those you love. Some, like Tiger Woods, say they worked their entire lives, so they deserve to enjoy all the surrounding temptations.

When Eva Longoria was asked about her divorce she replied, "It wasn't about whom he chose. I had moments of like: okay, I'm not sexy enough? I'm not pretty enough? Am I not smart enough? Then I immediately stopped. Don't start doing that because you can get stuck in that cycle and carry that into other things." In your relationships, as in your career, don't play the compare game. It's deadly.

If you have an affair with a married person and get discovered, take responsibility for your actions, but only your actions and not the subsequent choices of the wedded partners. Kristen Stewart was exquisitely eloquent when photographs revealed her smooching married director Rupert Sanders. Dating Robert Pattinson at the time, Stewart issued a public apology, "This momentary indiscretion has jeopardized the most important thing in my life, the person I love and respect the most, Rob. I love him, I'm so sorry." Sanders and Liberty Ross, his wife of ten years, split six months later. While the relationship with Stewart was likely the proximate cause, the infidelity was a symptom of something already amiss, and once exposed, the couple was unable to come to terms with the damaged relationship. Stewart and Sanders took responsibility in their own ways, but neither is responsible for the other's actions.

A split affects a lot of people, especially children. If you have children, help them positively deal with the breakdown of your relationship if that happens. Do everything you can, within reason, to ensure your split won't be nasty. Whether it is or isn't, co-parent in a way that benefits your kids rather than adds insult to injury. The upset in the family dynamic is trying and emotional enough as it is. Never use children as pawns where child custody or financial settlement issues are concerned. Think long and hard about the consequences of your actions, keeping the best interests of your children, long and short tem, as priority. In an interview with Charlie Rose, Johnny Depp said that his children handled the split between he and his longtime partner, Vanessa Paradis, well because as a couple they were committed to being honest.

Break-ups are costly. One of the most expensive Hollywood divorces was between Mel Gibson and his wife of 30 years, Robyn Gibson. Mother of their seven children, Robyn was awarded half of Mel's fortune, estimated to be as high as $850 million. Neil Diamond and Marcia Murphey divorced in 1975. Murphey left the marriage with $150 million. Amy Irving and Stephen Speilberg split in 1985. Irving walked away with $100 million. Diandra Douglas received $45 million upon her divorce from Michael Douglas in 2000. Linda Hamilton left with $50 million when she and James Cameron split in 1999. Phil Collins' divorce from Orlanne Cevey in 2003 cost him nearly $47 million. Heather Mills walked away with a cool $48.6 million when she and Paul McCartney divorced. Kevin Costner's divorce from Cindy Silva in 1994 cost around $80 million. And all that doesn't include all of the attorney fees. Top celebrity divorce lawyers earn $750 per hour and more.

If you're considering marriage, bone-up on pre-nups. Those who haven't drafted such legal documents paid a hefty price for their omission. Kelsey Grammar didn't have one when he married Camille Donatacci. He didn't feel the need for one because, as a result of a series of bad business decisions and a drug problem, Grammar was nearly broke at the time. His financial fortune improved considerably during his 14-year marriage. Donatacci was awarded half of their $60 million net-worth in the divorce settlement. California, where many celebrity unions occur, is a community property state. If you're married, pay attention to how and where your money flows. As with your financial advisers, never blindly entrust your good fortune to another.

Penny Douglas Furr, family law attorney, CNN commentator, and frequent guest on the Nancy Grace Show, consults with me on numerous occasions to understand nuances of behavior within some of her high-profile clients. In these conversations, and without namedropping, she's expressed how difficult it is to keep private divorce details private. She said there are always people at the law offices and courts who stand to make a lot of money if they break confidentiality and sell the juicy details of your break-up to the media.

All a reporter has to do is find one person in a desperate situation that is willing to take the risk. Be very careful about trashing your partner because those allegations will go into the pleading and other papers filed with your case. Even if those documents are sealed, there are always ways to violate that order from the inside. Secretaries, receptionists, office manager, paralegals, computer specialists, and other office personal do not have to have a bar license that can be revoked if confidentiality is breeched.

Furr advises that before you file a lawsuit, try to mediate privately with the other side so that what's publicly filed is minimal. Typically, mediation is a process that requires the involvement far fewer people. When the divorce is handled quickly and out of the public courts, it is easier to uphold secrecy in your personal matters.

When the deal is done, give yourself time to process the end of your relationship. Escaping into another relationship while carrying the baggage from a previous one may destine you to rebound hell. And the media will ardently report every episode of your impetuous flight. Most ricochet relationships fizzle within a few months. Make better use of that time re-establishing a healthy connection to your most important relationship: the one you have with yourself. Feed your soul instead of your fear.

One of the best ways to deal with a breakup is to throw yourself into your work. By staying focused on your career, and the responsibilities that go with it, you have less time to get caught up on the real and emotional aftermath. Rely on your support team. Good friends who know you well will provide an anchor to the upheaval in your circumstance. When you're calm and collected, take stock of the relationship. What did you learn? What would you have done differently? What will you do differently in the future? What positive benefits did you—and still—receive as a result of the union? Look closely: the good stuff is there. You wouldn't have been in the relationship for more than a nanosecond if you weren't getting something you wanted out of it. Without judgment, own your role in the meltdown of what was once a solid understanding. Don't play the blame game or bash your ex to the media or your children. Doing so will only make you look bitter and petty. Instead, let the facts speak for themselves as you keep private matters private.

When you do meet the next love of your life, make sure you're enamored by their true presence rather than promise of their persona.

Chapter Five
The Business of Fame

To become a celebrity is to become a brand name.
– Philip Roth

The minute you're not learning I believe you're dead.
– Jack Nicholson

A celebrity name is never enough for an intelligent mass market. Truly successful businesses are born of passion and heartfelt interest.

– Elle Macpherson

You *ARE* Your Brand
(Whether You Like It or Not)

Building a viable brand persona is a business. Some in the industry resist the development of business acumen because they think it will restrain creative talent. That simply isn't true. The ability to run your career efficiently as a business is what will give you more opportunities to do what you love to do creatively and make a good living while doing it. Face it: you're an entrepreneur. You might as well be a good one.

While there are fundamental questions to answer and systems to implement for every successful business, not all entrepreneurs are alike in how they think about and run their business. The primary differentiation is *mindset*, or the view you adopt for yourself and the way you lead your life and business.

If you believe that your qualities are set in stone, then you have what is called a *fixed mindset*. Those with a fixed mindset seek to prove themselves over and over again—whether they realize it or not. Every situation is evaluated with one or more of these questions:

- Will I succeed or fail?

- Will I look smart or stupid?

- Will I be accepted or rejected?

191

• Will I feel like a winner or a loser?

As such, those with a fixed mindset will evaluate their opportunity to succeed from a fixed starting point with no ability to learn or to improve going forward. They tend to talk themselves out of opportunities to expand because deep down inside they don't feel capable of successfully achieving anything greater than the level of what they've accomplished in the past. Fixed mindset people unknowingly create new situations that prove their fixed beliefs. In other words, a fixed mindset reinforces perceived limitations.

Those who believe that their basic qualities are things that can be developed and enhanced through their efforts have a *growth mindset*. They know that they can grow, change, and evolve with passion, training, practice, and a commitment to their goals. The willingness to stretch beyond comfort zones and the ability to stick to desired goals even when things are not going well are hallmarks of a growth mindset. In order words, a growth mindset bypasses perceived limitations and transforms situations into abilities and opportunities.

The good news is that if you discover that you fall into the fixed mindset category, you can transform your mindset into one that will allow you to evolve. Here are 3 tips to help you do just that:

1. Embrace Challenge

Be willing to see challenges as opportunities to learn and grow. Sometimes people with a growth mindset will stretch themselves so far that they do what was once thought of as impossible. People with growth mindsets live in a world of possibilities rather than impossibilities. There is always an easy reason to think something can't be done. That's just an excuse, most of the time. Try it first. Really work at it. Think about a time when you fully embraced a challenge. Even if you tried and failed, you had a chance to discover something new.

2. Find the Gold in Your Mistakes

Growth and expansion aren't achieved without making mistakes along the way. The key is to make new mistakes rather than merely repeat the same mistakes of the past. There is a gift in every mistake. It's the lesson that can be learned. Without judgment, fault, blame, or shame, examine the error. What thoughts did you have that lead to what decisions or choices, which lead to what actions, that created the unwanted outcome? Once you identify the role you played in creating the mistake, you have the information you need to make a different and better choice/action the next time around. As Albert Einstein once said, "We cannot solve our problems with the same thinking we used when we created them." New, more informed, ways of thinking would achieve a different and better results.

3. Examine Your Successes

As with evaluating your mistakes to reap the reward of the lesson learned, analyzing your successes will also give you a gift that keeps on giving. Ask yourself: what thoughts did you have that lead to what decisions, or choices, that lead to what actions, that created the wanted outcome? Once you identify the role you played in creating the successful outcome, you have the recipe to create similar successes over and over again. For example, if you nailed a late-night talk show interview, examine how, exactly, you did that. You might have thought about the interview ahead of time and come up with 2 or 3 prepared things to say that would be entertaining and engaging. Perhaps you did some homework to learn something interesting and timely about the host that you could leverage. Let's say you made sure, or had your publicist make sure, that you arrived in plenty of time, so you didn't feel rushed before you had to go on camera. Maybe you made time for yourself during the day so that you could show up to the interview replenished, calm, and focused. In this examination, you now know what to do to nail your next interview and the one after that.

Observe and Champion Your Mindset

Thankfully, perseverance is a great substitute for talent.

– Steve Martin

It's not just your business savvy and talent that will secure your success. The foundations upon which you base your choices upon play a critical role. Take a moment to think about how you think. Do you have a fixed or a growth mindset? If you have a fixed mindset, chances are you're frustrated or depleted as you struggle with some areas of your business. If you have a growth mindset, you're energized and motivated even if you're facing a challenge.

You have everything you need already within you to transform a mindset that stunts your growth into one that empowers you to thrive in every area of your life. Take the time each day to observe where you acted with a fixed mindset and where you expressed a growth mindset. The more you shift from a fixed to a growth mindset, the more you'll develop a renewed resilience that will become the foundation of your sustained, successful business.

In addition to having a mindset of a champion, good business people know that it's not the size of the enterprise that's important. It's the size of the profit. If you're spending more than you're making, you have an expensive hobby rather than a business. A healthy and sustainable profit will go a long way to give you the creative freedom you want for years to come.

It's time to make some really important decisions about the business side of your fame. It's vital to make investments in certain aspects of your brand persona before it is apparently needed. You have to invest in the right team structure and the right team members. This is what builds the foundation for sustainable growth.

The business of celebrity is to appreciate value through amplified public appreciation. Fame is a process, a journey, not an event. Not all paths are equal. Once you make it, you have to continue to invest a lot of time, energy, and resources to stay on top and leverage your success. You're a star because the public has placed that value upon you. You give them something they want and they invest their time, energy, and money into your brand.

Become a visionary of your celebrity value. Fame has become an ideological and intellectual framework in modern capitalism. When monetized prudently, it has the potential to increase in value, earning dividends for you in multiple ways, some of them quantifiable and others intangible. Invest your celebrity currency to grow your personal and professional worth. Make hay while you're in the spotlight because, just as day is followed by night, you can be sure that you'll not always be occupying center stage. This is the capricious nature of fame's fate.

There are those who are famous for being famous, and those who put their fame to work and thrive. There are celebrities who fritter away their fame indiscriminately in meaningless self-indulgent activities, and there are celebrities who take advantage of their fame when it is at its prime and in it invest. The former are oblivious to the wheel of fame and fortune as it spins, while the latter recognizes the special status that fame bestows on them to reap rich benefits that continue to endear them to fans and also bring returns long after their fame starts to wane.

There are movie, media, and showbiz stars with fans that love to applaud or sportspersons performing in top form whose following increases with every new performance record that they achieve. This is merely allowing fame to take its natural course of action. However, when the popularity that a celebrity enjoys in her or his own area of specialization is taken beyond its natural influence and applied to other activities and spheres of business in a systematic and deliberate fashion, then fame starts to function like a business enterprise. The objective is to derive not only quantifiable returns but also spread and engender a reputability that continues to grow and benefit you as a celebrity *and* as a business entity.

There are many celebrities who have built an entire industry in response to the encouragement of their fans, either through tangible products and services that they endorse or through products that they market under their own brand name. This parallel business continues to grow and expand in value and most often provides additional momentum to the popularity of the celebrity. The persona and the brand work in symbiosis to create a self-sustaining enterprise.

Justin Timberlake became the new Creative Director for the Bud Light Platinum brand on the heels of the announcement that BlackBerry named singer Alicia Keys as their Global Creative Director. Rather than be paid to appear in an ad with the product, these stars are compensated for their creative direction of the marketing, ushering a new paradigm for celebrity endorsements.

As a celebrity, your name commands massive attention, interest, and profit-generating value. While you are paid for your hard work, you are also the sourced financial asset to those who stand to gain from the commercialization of your brand persona. A premium is paid for your star power.

Multifaceted complex industries influence the growth, expansion, and circulation of a celebrity brand. Endorsements and public appearances are just the tip of the iceberg. There is an unbelievably rich business resource that lies latent and untapped within you as a celebrity.

Make no mistake: while you are an individual, your persona is a brand. As a brand, you must run your business effectively and efficiently with excellence. There is an equity and economy of celebrity when your brand becomes a commodity that can be capitalized. As a product, there is intellectual property in your image that must be protected in order to retain its value. While your focus is on the further development of a viable, abundantly profitable career, your name and image will be used to make a lot of other people rich. You'll be used to market films, television programs, newspapers, magazines, clothing and accessories, health and beauty products, and everything else under the sun. Celebrity endorsements, real or implied, associate a brand with the attributes of your persona.

If you're hired to endorse a particular product, be seen using the product. Do not be out and about in public cheating with a competitive brand. Luxury watch brand Raymond Weil paid Charlize Theron to wear only his watches for two years. During this period, Theron also had a contract with Dior perfume and was publicly seen wearing a Dior watch an event. She also broke her contract with the brand when she wore other jewelry in an ad for charity, another contractual no-no.

Jessica Simpson partnered with The Tarrant Apparel Group to create the inexpensive JS by Jessica Simpson and Princy Jeans and apparel collections. Simpson refused to wear the cheap clothes in public appearances. She also revealed to a reporter that her favorite brand of jeans was True Religion instead of her own Princy label. Make sure you understand the impact of and agree to every requirement in your endorsement agreements.

The holy grail of endorsements is when products are developed based solely on your identity. Perhaps the most successful is Nike's Air Jordan line of athletic shoes, leveraging pro-athlete Michael Jordan's global star power. Despite the fact that Jordan retired in 2003, Air Jordans are still the top selling model for many sneaker retailers. They reinforce and maintain the values associated with the Jordan's image, which includes quality and performance.

One of the main reasons this product branding was so successful is because the attributes of the sneaker mirrored the attributes of Michael Jordan's public image. If the public sees a disconnection between the branded product and the brand, they're liable to reject the product. Putting your name on too many products will also make you seem like a sell-out, a person who's already wealthy and who will do anything just to make even more money. In this case, less is certainly more.

Agents, managers, publicists, stylists, financial advisors, producers, and various other service providers to the stars have a vested interest in your market value. Unlike a traditional innate product, your brand is ever fluid as the interests of the masses shift and as you exercise your free will each and every day. If your star wanes in the public sphere, so does your economic value throughout the chain—beginning with your own earning capacity.

Have no illusions about it. The environment of fame is not a playground; it's serious business. Making fame work for you isn't much different from managing any other type of business. Your personal and commercial interests must be masterfully managed and vigorously protected. Like any business, a carefully considered brand strategy must be developed and aligned with the attributes and values that make up the brand image. These attributes and values serve the brand best when rooted in the authenticity of the individual. Like any other type of enterprise that wants to sustain success, you'll need a marketing plan, a system for modifying and improving your brand image, and a strategy for building and maintaining consumer loyalty. The daily march of your business machine becomes a delicate dance when you factor in the critical importance of your personal happiness and sense of fulfillment.

If you're a pro-athlete, you're used to your performance in the game being minutely scrutinized. Your skills are bought and sold in the pro-sports marketplace. While you may be used to having your body banged, bruised, toned, punished, and assaulted as you reached for the gold in your sporting discipline, you may not be ready for the imperious manipulation and molding of your commoditized brand image. As a top athlete, you can expect about two-thirds of your yearly salary to be earned through a variety of product and service endorsements. Keep your winning reputation intact, you'll continue to realize substantial income through brand associations beyond retirement as a pro. A sportsperson who is ranked number one for his or her performance in the field has the right the command a certain premium for endorsements and from other forms of monetizing their celebrity status. The transient nature of fame means capitalizing on opportunities as and when they occur so that the highs and lows average out in the longer term.

Maintain a balance between how much your fame is worth and

how much of the potential for your fame to earn is being utilized. Too much or too less of an emphasis on capitalizing your fame can influence your professional career as well as your future prospects. A singer or an actor needs to recognize that his or her performances on the stage (and off it) are interlinked with the business potential of fame. To borrow a clichéd metaphor, capitalizing on fame is like stretching an elastic band. Let it go lax and it not only is a waste, but it is in poor form and it can adversely affect your celebrity status. Stretch it too far and it could reach a breaking point where your value can take a nosedive—not to mention hurting your reputability and how your fans perceive you.

Be professional. The only people who get away with being difficult are those who are either critical to a project or who can afford to be thrown out on their derrieres. Whining, bitching, complaining, and blaming will get you noticed, but the demands won't advance you're career.

What you once took care of for yourself is now largely in the hands of others. Your image, clothes, shopping, professional and artistic direction, and schedule are overseen by those who are in the business of taking care of such things. These delegates are in the business of getting your needs met while making a profit for themselves. A lot of people will want a piece of your assets. A lot can be lost as well as gained. The job remains with you to be practical, so question everything and make your own decisions. Read and understand contracts. Get a good lawyer and accountant, one you've thoroughly vetted and trust, and never be afraid to ask them to explain it to you simply. Have them break it down for you until you understand what it is you're signing. Learn what makes a successful business and brand successful. Above everyone, trust yourself.

Your star power opens the door to lots and lots of opportunities. You get offers, some more lucrative than others, each and every day. Discern which ones advance and enhance your brand value. When considering projects if you have to do *one for the mortgage*, follow it up by doing *one for the soul*. No less than Steven Spielberg famously said that he desperately wanted to do *Schindler's List*, but to get that project going, he had to make *Jurassic Park* "for the mortgage." Sometimes even the one for the mortgage isn't such a chore (though the one for the soul won seven Oscars—the mortgage only won three!).

Keep your agreements. How you value keeping your word largely reflects the value of your reputation. While contracts are essential, your handshake and word is as good as a contract if you want to be the kind of person with whom people want to do business. What kind of person are you? Do you stand by your agreements? How about the casual agreements you make with friends? Those count when it comes to your ability to keep your word. If you readily break your word with people you care about, you'll find justifications to break your word in your contractual agreements. If you can't keep an existing agreement, make a new agreement that serves the best interests of everyone involved.

Your Peeps

With fame, you can't trust everybody. You can't depend on them for being there for you as a person. They will only be there because of what you've got and what you can bring to their life. It's not a relationship—it's a leech.

– Chris Brown

No longer is a celebrity posse a symbol of star power. The size of a trailing entourage is now viewed as the depth of a star's desperation. The biggest and most enduring stars, such as Tom Hanks, just like to blend in without making a fuss. The bigger the entourage, the greater the opportunity to have your dirty laundry exposed virally.

As an in-demand person, your image is a business. You need a team of professionals to keep the business operating efficiently, effectively, and optimally. As the CEO, you have the ultimate responsibility to inspire a high quality level of performance from your staff. Note that I said inspire, not beat or frighten them into submission. Collectively and individually, they have the power to uplift or wreck havoc with your brand.

When you hire, hire the best. Make sure each member of your entourage is road-tested, not star-struck. Execute strict confidentiality agreements. You don't want anyone hitting the money mother lode by selling your dirty laundry—literally and figuratively.

Tell-all books are grabbed up like peanuts at a ballpark. Princess Diana's former butler, Paul Burrell, reportedly earned about $500,000 for spilling the intimate details of her private life in the palace. Christopher Gaida, award show A-lister escort, wrote a tell-all titled

Arm Candy: A Celebrity Escort's Tales From The Red Carpet, where he reveals secrets the starts would rather keep hushed. Lance Armstrong's personal assistant, Mike Anderson, wrote a brutal expose for *Outside* magazine where he painted a very unflattering portrait of his former boss. He outed the fallen Tour de France winner's under-the-table cash deals, avoidance of world Anti-Doping Agency testers, and leaving his wife in an abrupt and cruel fashion.

Scott Rudin, legendary and multiple award winning producer of *The Truman Show*, *The Hours*, *Zoolander*, and *Closer*, was nailed by many of his ex-assistants who publicly shared their abusive experiences with his unforgiving management style. Rudin was described as a cross between Attila the Hun and Miss Jean Brodie. He holds the unofficial crown of Hollywood's most feared boss, according to the *Wall Street Journal*.

The magazine, *In Touch*, interviewed several nannies-to-the-stars who bared their secrets. While not all of the juicy items were negative in nature, they still revealed private personal moments that were meant to remain unshared. Sara Trumble, nanny to Heather Mill's daughter, aired the laundry of the *Dancing On Ice* star. Daisy Wright, nanny to the children of Jude Law while he was engaged to Sienna Miller, spilled the beans about her affair with Law after Wright caught them in bed together. People who live in your house can rifle through your most private drawers, stealing and selling your unmentionables.

Establish and enforce strict confidentiality policies with anyone and everyone who has access to your personal and private information. While you're at it, have your spouse sign a non-disclosure agreement. Jude Law's first wife, actress Sadie Frost, penned a memoir titled *Crazy Days* about her tumultuous marriage and her battle with depression. Reality star Linda Hogan published an autobiography chronicling her volatile marriage to wrestler Hulk Hogan. She accused her ex of abuse, claiming she was afraid he would kill her. Actor Dean McDermott's ex-wife, Mary Jo Eustace, wrote *Divorce Sucks: What to Do When Irreconcilable Differences, Lawyer Fees and Your Ex's Hollywood Wife Make You Miserable*. McDermott had an affair with Tori Spelling during his marriage to Eustace. Spelling and McDermott later married. Mia Farrow wrote a scorching revelation about Woody Allen. Bobby Brown dissed Whitney Houston. I could go on. You get the idea.

Okay, back to your entourage: know the going rate for each category of support service. Pay your people well and within the standard range of compensation. Communicate your appreciation for their service. While they work hard to facilitate the glamour of your image, the work isn't glamorous. It's most often an arduous life where 20-hour workdays are common. Treat your staff with the respect, and they will rise to the occasion. How you treat others is reflected in how you are perceived, and when dealing with image, perception is everything.

Since you will be spending quite a bit of time with your key staff, it's essential that there's compatibility and genuine support for one another. While friendly, keep the relationship professional. You are the boss. They are highly valued employees. I'll first list your key personal and business "go-to peeps," and then I'll go into more detail about the key members of your inner circle. I'll remind you over and over again (because it bears repeating): prepare and execute confidentiality agreements with everyone who is in a position to learn your confidences.

Top 5 Entourage Staff You Do NOT Need

You do not need assistants to wipe your brow, carry your special toilet paper, hand you towels, carry your umbrella, taste your food, dress your dog or kiss your ass.

Reportedly, the following celebrities employ these "necessary" members of their entourage:

1. Justin Bieber: Pizza and diet coke holder
2. Mariah Carey: Breast tape wrangler
3. Ludacris: Game Boy battery changer
4. Jennifer Lopez: Shoe caretaker
5. Prince Charles: Shoelace ironer

Now what I'm about to say may sound contradictory. I assure you it isn't. We all have things we don't need. That doesn't make us bad people. Consider that employing a personal shoelace ironer and the like isn't a good or a bad thing. A shoelace ironer irons shoelaces. Period. A shoelace isn't good or bad. An ironer isn't good or bad. These are just things. What determines whether or not something is good or bad is the emotional relationship you have with it.

If, for example, you have a shoelace ironer because you're giving someone a job (and you can easily afford to) who wouldn't otherwise have an occupation, then you have a healthy relationship with that position. If, however, you engage a person to iron your shoelaces to make yourself feel more important, then you have an unhealthy relationship around the employment of a shoelace ironer. There isn't a shoe, lace, or ironer in the world that can make you feel important for more than a nanosecond. Significance, like every other emotion, is an inside job.

Take a look at the people around you. What purpose do they serve…really? Rigorously challenge your inner *status quo* to discern whether or not you've created a healthy, or unhealthy, brand environment. Like with unwanted love handles, trim the fat. You'll look and feel better.

The buck stops with you. Even if you have a manager to manage your team, you are your manager's manager. Lead your team to stay upright and on course. Purge bad behavior. Karma's only a bitch if you are. An unethical boss models behavior that will be eventually mirrored by the staff. An unfair boss is a powerful de-motivator. The buddy boss is powerless. The disorganized boss cannot lead. The entitled boss translates personal fame into controlling (vs. inspiring) power. Lead your team by hiring the best, those that are team players who take the initiative. Give them the tools to do their job well. Trust them in how they choose to get the job done. Offer constructive feedback instead of criticism. Encourage their suggestions for growth and improvement.

The Entourage You WILL Need

Your personal staff (depending upon your individual needs) are the people who are going to keep you…well, going. They are going to help you achieve your best self, your career goals, and meet your daily needs. You are bigger than just you, now, and while you certainly don't need to overdo it, you definitely will need some help. These people are appropriate to your new status, and it's good to have them on your payroll:

Your Daily Associates

Personal Assistant: An initiative driven multitasking energizer-bunny wizard. To support some high-profile celebrities and executives, this can easily become an on-call 24/7 commitment. It's a stressful job, so allow your assistant the time to replenish. Your personal assistant is not your therapist.

Stylists: To craft your persona's style and make you look always fabulous styling your clothing, makeup, and hair. These people are also not your therapists.

Nanny: If you have children. You are still the parent. Value your child enough to invest your time and energy with each child every day. The nanny is not your maid.

Personal Trainer or Yogi: Your accountability partners for or fitness and possibly nutrition support. Your trainer or yogi is not your therapist.

Security/Bodyguard: Must be disciplined, consistent and well trained. He is not there to hold your purse.

Chauffeur: May be live-in, depending upon the level of service required.

Private Chef: This can be a high stress position, especially if live-in.

Therapist or Psychiatrist: A professional therapist who treats you behaviorally if you suffer from psychological challenges (or are in a recovery program) or a professional psychiatrist who specializes in the diagnosis and medical treatment of a mental illness.

Your Business Advocates

Manager: Champions your career. A manager is fully vested in your success because his or her success depends upon yours. Rarely bound to agency and state rules.

Agent: State licensed to get you work. Commission based between 10-15%. Prioritizes client roster based on the most likely to generate lucrative fees, fast and often. A bad agent is worse than having no agent at all.

Publicist: Generates and manages your publicity. Her job is to preserve and promote your special mojo. Well connected especially with those in the media who can place your story.

Mentor: To keep you grounded, admired, and inspired as you navigate the promise and pitfalls of fame, fortune, and freedom. A mentor is not a therapist or psychiatrist who doles out pharmaceuticals for inner angst.

The following pages provide more details on the most imperative members of your entourage.

Personal Assistant

I don't have an assistant. I make a lot of people around me my slaves, but no assistant.
— *Shirley MacLaine*

You're a busy person with a life that gets bigger and busier. The more you have, the more complicated your life will become and you'll need someone you can unequivocally As an overscheduled individual, a personal assistant (PA) who will assist you in your daily business and personal tasks is a practical hire. Depending upon your unique needs, the role of your assistant can be varied from answering calls, scheduling meetings, and handling your correspondence to arranging travel, running errands, shopping, paying bills, purchasing gifts, remembering birthdays, and everything in between. You must trust your PA to help you manage it all. He or she will have access to your credit cards, social security numbers, secrets, insecurities, pet peeves, personal and career agenda, house, car, dirty laundry, basically your life matters.

The personal assistant industry has blossomed over the last several years, and finding qualified experienced professionals has become big business in and of itself. What was once the exclusive domain of celebrities and pro-athletes is now expanded into the world of executives, philanthropists, politicians, dignitaries, socialites, and successful entrepreneurs.

A good experienced personal assistant who takes the initiate to anticipate your needs doesn't come cheap. Hiring the wrong person can be costly. Assistants generally earn between $60,000 and $80,000 a year. Those who work tirelessly for an A-list star make on average

$120,000 to $150,000 annually, plus perks.

I met Deon Lowery, a highly revered PA and a top Executive Personal Assistant to an Executive at Sony Pictures Entertainment, on a plane as I was returning to Los Angeles from a conference on purposeful financial planning in Denver. At the time, Lowery was an Executive Assistant to a young billion dollar Beverly Hills heiress and her husband. Lowery was in charge of running the household, an army of staff and responding to perpetual demands. He has also served as Personal Assistant to high-profile personalities such as top criminal defense attorney Donald Etra, with affiliates such as George Bush, Rihanna, Snoop Dogg, and various other celebrities and top public officials.

Several months later while sitting at a café table under the trees on the Sony lot, Lowery explained the nuances between working as a PA to a wealthy individual or celebrity and working as an Executive Personal Assistant within a corporate environment. We also discussed the responsibilities of his job, the challenges he's seen and experienced, and the optimal environment for a productive, efficient, and mutually supportive working relationship between a PA and his employer.

In the private sector, Lowery has experienced the good and the downright nasty when it comes to employer personalities and demands. The best of the best work to build a mutually trusting relationship and is clear about expectations. The worst of the worst displayed no respect for people in general, treating employees and service providers as lesser human beings. Money was used as a free pass to be verbally abusive and confrontational. Ironically, it seemed the more a star's popularity began to fade, the ruder and insulting became the behavior.

211

I'll speculate that you want to get the best PA, you develop a long-term, reciprocally rewarding working relationship. In order to do that, you have to know how to engage what will best serve your needs. Based on what I gleaned from Lowery, my clients, and other interviews, the following will give you some guidelines on how to hire, motivate, and lead your PA.

What you're really looking for is a professional partner. Don't even think about hiring a friend or relative for this position because it will be hard to establish and maintain the boundaries of employer and employee. While on rare occasions the dynamic works, usually it becomes a nightmare. More importantly, only consider applicants who have a lot of experience as a PA and are able to provide verifiable references. Only interview prospects that meet essential criteria.

Before you interview anyone, get clear on what an ideal PA would be for you. First and foremost, you want someone you can trust completely. You want someone who is loyal, dependable, and absolutely reliable. Meticulous organizational skills are a must. If you travel internationally, it is essential that whomever you hire be knowledgeable in booking such trips as well as time and security differences in each country. An experienced PA will already have a domestic and international database of contacts to leverage in his position.

Notice how your potential PA arrives for the interview. Is she on time? Is she prepared? Does her appearance reflect someone who will represent you well? What is the "vibe" you get when you first meet her? Does she look you in the eye with confidence? Is her energy level high or anemic?

Begin with some brief pleasantries to establish rapport before you dive right into the main purpose conversation. Your interviewee will likely know the job description and already have a sense of who you are if she's done her homework. What she doesn't know are your expectations in a PA. Articulate exactly what you expect of the role and of the relationship. You'll only waste your time and hers if you hold back on explaining everything you expect your PA to be able to deliver. Both of you deserve to be able to make an informed decision about whether and not the engagement would be a good fit. Also let her know if and how the position will evolve over time.

If you want someone you can trust, for example, just because she's listed "trustworthy" as one of her resume attributes, dig deeper. How does she define trust? Ask her to give you examples of how she was trustworthy in her former positions. If you want her to be available to you full-time, get on the same page about what "available full-time" means. It's important that she's able to take the initiative to anticipate your needs so ask her, specifically, how's she's done that for others in the past. You also want a problem solver, a fire putter-outer, so elicit examples of how she's risen to those occasions.

Ask her what attitudes and character she regards most to determine whether or not you share common values. Ask her how she sees herself fitting into the position. Get to know the person she is beyond the resume. Invite her to ask you any questions she may have that are relevant to the job.

When you've completed your round of interviews hire the finest of the finest. It's worth it if you have to pay her a little more because an experienced, reputable, principled, meticulous, responsible, level-headed, and honest professional partner will give you priceless peace of mind. You don't want to have to find a replacement and go through the process of retraining. Upon selection and acceptance, execute and honor employment contracts and confidentiality agreements.

The first day together will set the tone of your working environment and relationship going forward. You're the employer, so it is up to you to lead. Begin the day with a review of responsibilities and expectations. Even though you hired someone exquisitely skilled at anticipating your desires, she is not a mind reader. Express your needs, wants, and outcomes you want to see per project and over the long-term. Identify absolute Do's and Don'ts. Communicate problems that need to be solved.

Identify your priorities so she can become a good gatekeeper and filter. The information will help her screen calls and know that she can break into your board meeting if there is an emergency with your child but not your freeloader cousin. If you told your PA you don't want to be interrupted if your spouse calls, inform your spouse of this policy. Your PA will know and manage your daily schedule to the minute. If you want your time to be valued, appreciate the time other people schedule with you. Be on time. Encourage your assistant to interrupt your meeting if you need to wrap it up to get to your next appointment

If you want your PA to trust and respect you, show that you trust and respect her. As a leader, set the example. Keep your word and confidences between you. Rather than intimidate, express and set boundaries. If your PA goes above and beyond in the accomplishment of her role, recognize the spectacular level of service with your words and a bonus of some sort. According to Lilit Marcus, New York-based author of the blog and book *Save The Assistants*, Sarah Jessica Parker gave her assistant so much credit for keeping things organized during the first *Sex and the City* movie that her assistant got an associate producer credit on the film.

Trust your PA to figure out the *how* when it comes to delivering results. That's her job. Ask about and give your PA the tools to get the job done—*and get out of her way*. Micromanaging wastes everyone's time and diminishes motivation. Introduce your PA to your partners, associates, service providers, friends, and family members with whom she will need to be in contact with in order to manage your affairs efficiently. Unless the job description specified that she is accountable to anyone else other than you, do not allow anyone else, including your spouse, to bark orders at her. Don't create a situation where your PA gets stuck in the middle of mixed priorities, confidences, and duties. You'll only make the working climate an uncomfortable and potentially compromising situation if she has to split her loyalties.

Openly and consistently acknowledge tasks well done. Offer constructive feedback when things need to be corrected or performed to a higher standard. There is a nifty little formula for providing a positive critique. It's called the "Sandwich Method." Look for and begin with the recognition of at least one or two aspects of the assignment that were done well. At the very least, your PA made some sort of an effort. Appreciate the intention. Then suggest "areas of growth," ways in which she can improve upon what was delivered. Seek to teach in a way that supports understanding rather than lecture disapprovingly. Wrap it up with a positive statement, perhaps something about your confidence in her ability to perform to your standards going forward.

Give your PA access to the areas of your life and work that is within her responsibility. In it's simplest terms, if you want her to go clothes shopping for you, let her look in your closet to fully acquaint herself with your sense of style and fashion preferences. If you want her to manage your email or use your computer, give her your passwords. Do not give your new PA the password to your banking and other sensitive information unless a higher level of trust is earned over time. Lowery didn't get the password to run financial statements from his boss until he was at least a year into the job.

While you may have delegated these tasks to your PA, it is still your responsibility to monitor what goes on, especially in critical areas. Never, ever, give passwords and other sensitive information to more than one PA under your employ. If there's a problem, it will be hard for you to discern who's ultimately responsible for a breech, as each will likely deny culpability. You'll have to fire them both and start the process all over again with new PAs. Communicate directions and tasks via email to give you a virtual track record of what you requested in case there is any confusion or misunderstandings about what you expect delivered.

Meet one-on-one with your PA at least once a week to go over your calendar, discuss anything that might have come up since you last met, and what's looking ahead, including any upcoming travel plans. This is a good time to discuss any issues in how you're working together and the job itself. Putting off such communication only leads to more trouble. Resolve problems through a conversation that is calm and solution-oriented.

As time goes on, the more responsibility you ask her to take on, the more you need to be prepared to pay for a PA who will be able to handle the extra work load and get the job done without lessening the quality of service. If your PA has served you well over the years and has a burning desire and talent as, say, a writer, do her a solid. Leverage your influence to help her land a suitable writing job when your time together has run its course.

Agent

Lots of people want to ride with you in the limo; but what you want is someone who will take the bus with you when the limo breaks down.

– Oprah

Your agent handles your career. An agent's fundamental goal is to fashion a star as a clearly separate economic presence distinct from any individual film, television show, or entertainment brand. She believes in your talent and marketability and uses all of her resources to keep you working and paid well. She'll send your headshots, resumes, and other promotional materials to casting directors and other business entities working to secure the best and most profitable deals. Defending, advocating, and promoting your best interests, she'll also secure the most supportive and comfy working environments possible.

Different regulations govern different types of agents that are established by various artists' unions and the legal jurisdiction in which the agent operates. There are also professional organizations that license talent agencies. In California, agencies must be licensed under special sections of the California Labor Code, which defines an agent as a "person or corporation who engages in the occupation of procuring, offering, promising, or attempting to procure employment for artists" because they work with highly lucrative contracts.

There are talent agencies that specialize in various disciplines. The different types of agencies include commercial, literary, voice-over, modeling, broadcast journalist, sports, music and more. While not a requirement, having an agent can open doors you can't penetrate on your own.

Hollywood's largest talent agencies, Creative Artists Agency (CAA), William Morris Agency, International Creative Management (ICM), United Talent Agency (UTA), and Endeavor, were known as the big five. In 2009, Endeavor and the William Morris Agency merged to form William Morris Endeavor (WME).

When there is big money to be made, scam artists lurk to take advantage of newcomers. If you're looking for an agent, do your homework. Research and meet with established agencies. No reputable agency charges for representation. They may suggest an investment for new photos or training. Beware of pay-to-play practices. Make sure you get your money's worth and have guarantees backed up in writing. Ask for references and referrals, information that you can personally check out. Ask to see proof of past bookings. It anything feels fishy, it probably is.

If you're an above-the-line talent who would like to read material from writers you admire, make sure your agent, your agent's assistant, and your assistant knows you will accept and read scripts offered by this select group. I've asked industry executives why a lot of great scripts never get made and one of the reasons offered is that scripts don't reach those who have the ability to get a picture made through their association. One screenwriter told me he was approached at a party by a big name actor who said he'd loved the writer's work and wanted to see his next script when it was finished. The screenwriter called one day to have the script delivered to the actor's agent only to be told by the very young assistant that unless the script came with an offer it would not be accepted for delivery or read. Some good scripts never reach the big screen because they get caught up in the many hierarchal layers of access.

When casting directors and producers send out breakdowns for their projects, they only send them to professional and known agents. Finding the right agent is critical, yet it's a decision that's often made without much consideration. You want to find the right agency. That agency meets your needs and your agent is the best person within that group to champion your career. Signing with an agent is only the beginning of the business relationships

Susan Simons, a highly regarded agent at David Shapira and Associates who has served on the Board of the Academy of Television Arts and Sciences as the Daytime Governor for three years, considers the dynamic between an agent and her client as a partnership. It's a marriage of sorts where she wants to represent her client as much as her client wants to be represented by her. Simons advises talent to be co-involved. Don't sit on the sofa eating bonbons expecting the agent to do everything. You have to be proactive about your career as well.

If you're busy working in a job, the last three weeks of the engagement are the most intense and you won't have time to look for anything new, yet that's the critical time when a new gig needs to get lined up. As a partner in the success of your career and livelihood, your agent will be the one looking for your next job so you can continue to focus on the one you have. She'll also negotiate it masterfully for you. Many agents have worked their way up from an entry-level position in the mailroom. They've learned to do's and don'ts along the way. An experienced agent can sing your praises and drive the deal much better than most people can when they represent themselves.

You will commit typically 10% of your fees to your agent, which is why agents are referred to as *ten percenters*. Simons was at a seminar when she heard an attendee balk at agents getting 10% of all fees even if a client got the job on his own. The reality of the agent/client dynamic is the agent, if he or she is delivering results, is keeping you in business for only 10% of the fee.

Some clients worry that if they bring in a lead on a job, the agent will submit other clients for that opening. Simons promises not to submit anyone else for that job unless told that the client isn't right for the gig. Only then will she offer anyone else from her roster. Keeping client submissions clean is paramount.

When it comes to choosing clients, Simons only represents people she really likes and respects. "It's a comfort level. I have to have a good feeling, feel a good vibe. It's all about my gut." Simons says some of her clients are so respectful that they email with a request to schedule a time to talk to her. She tells them to, "Just pick up the phone. This is a partnership and we're in it together." Simons' endless days and brutal schedule is worth it. Moving clients up to a higher credit level is her greatest joy.

Manager

My old manager of the Irish National Theatre said, "Don't worry about being a star, just worry about being a working actor. Just keep working." I think that's really good advice.

– Colm Meaney

Your Manager, if you choose to have one, will guide your career. A Manager differs from an Agent in that he might advise the client about brand development strategies, personal decisions, oversee the day-to-day business affairs, staff and other necessary tasks a busy client doesn't have time or specific knowledge to handle independently, but managers don't book jobs or make contract deals. A manager may collaborate with the publicist as his or her contact list may differ and add value to the mix. I've had a few band managers I know in the music industry tell me, *it's a fucking babysitting job*, when referring to clients who are known for their childish behavior and irresponsible reputations.

There are celebrity management companies who provide comprehensive celebrity brand services that include endorsement management, portfolio management, digital presence management, strategic public relations, interviewing techniques, grooming, and etiquette advice. Some of these companies specialize in specific categories, such as pro-athletes. Sports management companies understand the nuances of sponsorships, licensing, merchandising, and sports marketing.

An ideal manager, in addition to his expertise and experience, has strong business acumen and the ability to create opportunities.

A dynamic personality and excellent communication skills are a must. Above all, you must have absolute trust in your manager. This trust must be earned. Do not hire lightly. Be vigilant in vetting your prospective manager. Spend some time with the top candidates. Pay attention if you sense any red flags or inconsistencies. Ask around about his or her reputation. As with your Agent, get references you can personally verify.

The roles and responsibilities vary slightly from industry to industry, as does the financial compensation. Fees are negotiated. A renegotiation date and clause is recommended because circumstances and responsibilities can vary greatly within a relatively short period of time.

Publicist

Buzz and the right publicist are not only important but crucial in show business.
– Halston

My biggest problem in my life is I'm cheap and I didn't hire a publicist. In every awkward interview, normally actors get these things scripted.
– Robert Pattinson

As you may have surmised, that's a conversation between two media professionals debating on the relative merits of two stories, deciding which should be featured as the cover story. You already know that smut triumphs over smarts. It's a foregone conclusion which story will be featured.

The highest ideals of the media may be to influence popular opinion by presenting objective facts and discerning the most important things you (as a media consumer) need to know, but you can't blame the media if the only thing that sells on supermarket shelves is gossip and gore. As any business enterprise in a capitalist economy, those in the media also are expected to make money and sensationalism *sells*.

Public relations play a central role in the successful sustainment of any business that depends upon public allegiance. Publicists help shape your brand's message and mission, developing it into more than just a sum of your talents and contributions. By presenting client interests, events, and activities as newsworthy, they paint portrait of what the celebrity is supposedly really like. These paid professional promoters orchestrate a constant production of candid photo opportunities and interviews to perpetually positively advance the brand while maintaining the enigmatic quality of a star.

Publicists and other handlers tell you where to be, what to wear, and what to say to build more conspicuous hype around you. That's their job. Those are sanctioned occasions. Sometimes they will encourage you to allow for unauthorized publicity where you can be candidly seen without prejudice. They'll allow just enough exposure to grant access to personal moments while still intent on presiding over your privacy.

The was a time when publicists maintained a lot of control over what images of and stories about you saw the light of day. If a publication ran an unflattering photo or quip about you, they'd never get any further material on you for their upcoming publications. Not so anymore. Now your publicist has a full time job of brand management, often having to do damage control for things you have and haven't done.

Monitoring your reputation on and offline is a critical task. As a star, you're prone to rumors and false accusations and sensationalized reporting. Second to you, your publicist is the next layer of defense in your reputation management. While publicists have always stewarded a client's image in newspapers, magazines, and television, they now have the arduous task to shore up your good name in blogs, online articles, and the increasing number of social networking sites. A negative nugget can go viral in seconds. The problem has become so large, it's created a new niche of professionals who work with or independently of your publicist as your brand reputation manager.

Publicists need lots of energy and the ability to think fast on their feet. They're constantly trying to figure out how to prevent and put out fires. A bad story, true or not, can result in a substantial loss of income. Brand associations, endorsements, and lucrative jobs can be lost over small incidents that snowball into big ordeals that taint a client's reputation. In its thirst for juicy gossip, much of the public doesn't discern between fact and fiction.

Publicists also have to be social media gurus. Now traditional media is responding to what's trending on the Internet, whether true or not. Fact checking has become a lost art, even with widely available fact-checking sites a single click away. Moreover, a lot of what use to be considered scandal sheet litter is now regarded as mainstream. There exists a plethora of media outlets, online and off, that offer scintillating gossip, some of it completely made-up. One of the more reputable is Harvey Levin's TMZ, an outlet with about 20 million viewers. TMZ is considered to be a legitimate source because it does investigate allegations. They also have a reputation in getting the story first.

In addition to privacy rights, you have publicity rights. The right of publicity recognizes the commercial value of your name or likeness. You have the right to control and profit from the value of your identity and persona.

As a celebrity, the interest in your public identity extends beyond the natural copyright interest in your physical appearance to encompass the fictitious persona you have carefully developed. The issue with regard to the right of publicity, then, isn't about whether you've been unfairly exposed to public view: it's about who will profit from the sale. Copyright has little use in protecting you against the paparazzi because you don't own the photograph that is exploited. The copyright generally vests with the photograph or with the publication who hired him to shoot you and/or the story involving you. For professional photo shoots, the best way to avoid copyright infringement problems is to establish a written agreement before the images are taken specifying who will own the copyright upon completion. Retain the maximum control you can negotiate.

Protection against exploitation under the right of publicity vests regardless of whether or not it is exercised during your lifetime. The burden is still upon you to prove non-consensual use of your name, image, or likeness for another's benefit, usually commercial through commercial appropriation under privacy law or through a violation of copyright law.

There's a fly in the ointment here, too. Courts have held that the use of a photograph or story without consent in connection with a legitimate news publication or even to advertise such a publication doesn't constitute an actionable appropriation. As journalistic content, the use of the material is protected by the newsworthiness defense even if it negatively impacts you or diminishes your credibility in some way. Moreover, commercial publication without compensation enables the media to benefit from your fame at no cost.

The flip side is the publicity the media offers is your friend by providing you career-enhancing events and free advertising opportunities. A good publicist will know and leverage these opportunities on your behalf. It is up to you to get the most out of these engagements.

And publicists are no longer limited to those whose image is their major cache. With the ubiquitous outlets to be seen and heard, one of the more unusual aspects of celebrity is the age of the celebrity CEO. Business leaders are elevated to voyeuristic worthiness.

Personal publicists wrangle their executive clients to make sure they remain seen as cool-cats instead of fat-cats to further establish a more gratifying consumer relationship. Nowadays, any level of notoriety can result in the need for a professional publicist to help both the individual and the associated brand.

If you're an above-the-line talent involved in a movie, you will become very familiar with the press junket as part of the territory. You'll enter the strange world where you and the film will be the subject of what seems like interviewing speed-dating style: sweltering lights, photographs, provocative, redundant, and inane questioning. Expect long, exhausting days where you have nearly the same conversation over and over again in the name of efficiency. If the film does well as a result, you do well.

It's best to maintain a clear goal and intention throughout the tedious ordeal. Know your talking points. Stay on purpose, no matter how bored or cranky you feel, how ridiculous the question, or how tired you are of the entire process. Keep your composure even if you feel compelled to throw your microphone in the reporter's face. If you act like an arrogant asshole, your behavior will become the story instead of your contribution to the film.

Consider actor Jesse Eisenberg's interview with Univision reporter Romina Puga to promote his role in *Now You See Me*. While Puga may have been an inexperienced reporter, Eisenberg easily threw her off-guard at the onset by taking issue with Puga calling his co-star Morgan Freeman simply "Freeman." Freeman? What are you on a baseball team with him? Don't call Morgan Freeman "Freeman" like you're on a little league softball team with him.

Eisenberg was brutal in the way he attacked Puga's esteem,

calling her the "Carrot-Top of interviewers," after the comedian Scott Thompson, better known as Carrot Top for his bright red hair, prop comedy, and self-depreciating humor. When Puga responded that she might cry at the insult, Eisenberg said, "Don't cry now. Cry after the interview is over."

While a formidable actor, Eisenberg gained nothing good as a result of the interview. His presence during the interview was seen as bullying or, perhaps worse, an awkward and juvenile attempt at flirting. Puga was given kudos for holding her own during what she termed as a self-esteem butchering conversation.

Without a script to rely on, you're prone to reveal your true colors are exposed through the way you act and the things you say when interviewed. Those who engage and connect the best with their fans, the media, and contemporaries tend to be down-to-earth and show up authentically. Know your subject matter. If you're in a period film or show, know something about the era. Keep the conversation animated and fresh laced with a sense of humor and humility.

Your publicist can only be as good as you allow her to be through your behavior. If you want to be liked, be likeable. Become a masterful communicator. The more confident and articulate you are in your expression, the more you'll be viewed as a remarkable and extraordinary influence. Exhibit friendliness, relevance, empathy, and realness. Share your vision and passion for your projects through candid remarks that provide a glimpse to the real spirit of the person behind the persona.

Professional Photographers

A thing that you see in my pictures is that I was not afraid to fall in love with these people.
— *Annie Leibovitz*

There is a difference between someone invading your home and being invited in for editorial or advertising purposes. Contracted photo shoots are vastly different than uncontrolled shutterbugs. You won't find professional portrait, advertising, or editorial photographers beating a path to your door early in the morning to snap you in your jammies (except for Véronique Vial, but she's lovely).

Some cultures believe that being photographed steals your soul. I prefer to think of professional portraits as an exquisite reflection of it. There's much more involved in capturing the essence of a person in an image than the technical and creative aspects of using a camera. What makes an engaging photograph has a lot to do with the relationship between the photographer and his or her subject.

How do I know this? My husband, Al Satterwhite, is such a photographer. I've heard him tell of what makes a great photograph, who he enjoyed working with, and what personalities he would never work with again. More than a few client bills included hidden pain fees to compensate for the undue suffering endured to do the job.

Your photographer will start the relationship with you by taking the time to build trust. Ideally, you want the photograph to capture and reveal something poignant about your personality. In a portrait photo shoot, your photographer is likely doing his best to become invisible so he can capture you candidly. Posed images are okay as standard press fodder. They do little to unmask your individuality and help your brand.

Be receptive to the direction made by your photographer. He's expertly skilled at getting the best photograph out of you. Trust her process. Be willing to open up. Relax as you reveal your more natural side. That's when the magic happens and they snap the "it" shot.

If you like working with a particular photographer, request him for your subsequent photo shoots. You're already comfortable with each other and there's already an established trust. Time won't be wasted getting to that point. The gesture is also a show of appreciation for their work and it's an efficient business choice on your part.

There was a go-to photographer in the glory days of the Hollywood Studio system that was revered by the studios and their stars named Murray Garrett. I had the pleasure of spending time with him. His aesthetic helped change the nature of Hollywood photography, shooting some of the first candid portraits of the stars at work and play. Using trust and a keen eye, Garrett forever captured the essence of the individuals that made up the Hollywood elite. Marilyn Monroe, Gary Cooper, Frank Sinatra, Cary Grant, Lauren Bacall, Lucille Ball, Debbie Reynolds, Robert Mitchum, Jimmy Durante, Bob Hope, Bing Crosby, Danny Kaye, Grace Kelly, Clark Gable, and Natalie Wood are just a few of the great legends of show business Garrett photographed in his early career.

I asked him what, besides his extraordinary talent, afforded him such a backstage all access passport to a private world reserved for only the dignitaries of "the biz." Garrett's response was simple. Trust, absolute trust between the star, the client or the studio, and himself. To illustrate how essential the role trust played, he told me a few stories from his heyday in the golden age of Hollywood.

Garrett was hired to photograph Van Johnson and Ann Miller. On this particular day, the two actors were rehearsing a dance routine on the set. Wary of how cameras can get in the way and bother, even cause harm to, his subjects, Garret crouched under the protection of a table to get the shot. When the film was developed he realized, "Oh my God, she's not wearing any panties!"

Garrett immediately knew he had a problem on his hands. If the photo or negative got into the hands of the wrong people, it wouldn't be good for the actors or the studio. This was in the days when actors were signed under contract with a studio. Garrett called up the senior level public relations person at MGM and said, "I have a photograph you need to see. I'm coming to see you tomorrow." The studio PR guy responded coarsely, thinking Garrett had something nefarious and hush money would probably be involved.

Garrett showed up the next day with the photo and negatives and said, "Here. You need to take these. I don't want them. I don't want to be responsible if they get out to the public." The studio executive grabbed the images and said, "OK, now what do you want?" Garrett replied, "Nothing but a good relationship with MGM. That's it." "Nothing?" he replied astonished. "Nothing." Garrett answered with finality. Garrett maintained a good relationship with the studio ever since. A photographer who didn't value trust above all else might have made another choice, potentially damaging the careers of many people.

Later, Garrett was hired to cover a large private birthday party attended by everyone who was anyone in Hollywood. Private people do private things in private. After a grueling 12-hour shooting day that ended in the wee hours in the morning, Garrett dragged himself home and into bed. Shortly thereafter his wife, Phyllis, woke him up and said, "Don't you hear the phone? It's ringing off the hook. There's a guy on the line who wants to talk to you."

Garrett forced himself awake and took the call. A guy named Lou was on the other end of the line. He offered Garrett $30,000 in cash for all the footage, including the negatives, he shot that night. Thirty thousand dollars was an incredible amount of money over 50 years ago. Garrett refused the offer and said the material was not for sale. Lou upped the ante and offered $50,000. Garrett told Lou, again, that he wouldn't sell the images. Lou demanded to know Garrett's price. Adamantly, Garrett told Lou to bug off and that he would never sell and hung up the phone.

Now Garrett was scared. Lou worked for *Confidential*, a quarterly periodical published in the early 1950s that was considered a pioneer in scandal, gossip, and exposé journalism. The rag was full of innuendo and allegations and became an instant success under the tagline "The Lid is Off." They were known to bribe anyone for information and became the catalyst in the ruination of many reputations. Garrett figured if they couldn't buy what they wanted, they would steal it by breaking into his house—and soon. The next day, Garrett rang up his good friend Henry Rogers, who later became a principal in the global public relations firm Rogers and Cowan, and had him hold onto the photos for safe keeping. Another photographer might have taken the deal and bought a beautiful home in Beverly Hills on the backs of the reputations of those who graced his lens, but by doing so, he would have sacrificed his own reputation. In the end, Garrett's choices led to a long and fruitful career as a professional photographer, graced with the confidences of his deep roster of celebrity clientele.

When you identify and work with a photographer, you can, trust the direction he or she gives you, the quality of the shoot, and the integrity of the photograph. As professionals, these photographers are skilled in getting the best out of you. They don't want to sign their name to a mediocre photograph. An instruction may sound a bit odd. Still, trust and go with it. Garrett relayed the following story on why a trusting dynamic is key during a shoot.

The assignment was to photograph English actor and novelist David Niven. Extremely popular, Niven appeared in nearly a hundred films and many shows for TV. You may remember him for his role as Sir Charles Lytton in the 1982 *Pink Panther* films directed by Blake Edwards. Niven confided in Garrett that he had difficulty smiling for a still camera. He had no problem smiling for motion picture films because the shot was fluid, more natural. Smiling in front of a camera that shot one frame at a time was uncomfortable for Niven. Garret said, "No problem. I know just the thing to help you. Say the word shit." Niven was aghast. Garrett said, "Just trust me."

Niven did and for the next thirty to forty minutes Niven found endless ways to say, "shit." A different smile naturally formed on his face with each utterance and Garrett was able to get more than he needed for the shoot. Everybody won. The images were spectacular.

Garrett has little patience for *prima donnas*. One came in the form of a fourteen year-old boy who was a member of a young singing trio. The kid wouldn't listen or cooperate. He kept acting out, making it impossible for Garrett to do his job. Finally, Garrett slammed the kid against the wall and told him he wouldn't tolerate his antics any more. Shocked at being disciplined, the youth got his act together enough to complete the shoot. Garrett refused to work with him, or anyone else like that, again. The kid went on to become an infamous record producer.

The stories Garrett told me about his experiences in the golden age of Hollywood could fill another book. I hope a biographer more talented than I will chronicle these tales so generations to come can get a unique behind-the-scenes glimpse of an era that will never be repeated again. Too much has changed. The studios no longer rule the industry or its stars. The public has unprecedented access and the violation of star privacy is *de rigueur*. There are benefits as well as dangers. The public gets what it wants, but security has never been more necessary.

Security

I don't need bodyguards. I'm from the South Bronx.
– Al Pacino

When you're the center of attention, you're more likely to be wooed, stalked, bashed or attacked. The public in today's celebrity culture maintains an inappropriate sense of ownership. While most citizenry observe from afar, there are still thousands of people who will boldly approach, grab, threaten, and even verbally and physically attack those they adore and abhor. A simple walk down a public thoroughfare can become quite frightening and intimidating. It's not safe to be among the crowds. Efficient, effective security is a must.

A security guard plays a serious role in your life and the safety of your family. You want to hire someone highly recommended with impeccable references. Engage someone you trust completely for the long-term. While you can hire a private security guard on an individual basis, most choose to go through a security firm that offers a wide range of protection services. While you are kept safe, you'll also want to find out who's been harassing you and why.

Your security should be licensed, bonded and insured in the state in which he or she does business. Verify credentials through outside sources. Make sure rigorous background checks are passed. Hire to the level of service you require. If you only need situational protection decline a firm that pads the bill by mandating you be given twenty-four hour coverage. Chose a firm that will serve your specific needs.

The dark side of fame includes the risk of being stalked or kidnapped. Jason R. Peyton stalked Jennifer Aniston for days on Sunset Boulevard, etching notes on her car. When found, he was in possession of a sharp object, duct tape, and love notes. Jen obtained a permanent restraining order. Stalker Livia Bistriceanu believed Leonardo DiCaprio is the father of Jesus. Placed on psychological hold twice, Bistriceanu claimed she and DiCaprio got married and she was carrying his child. DiCaprio received a temporary restraining order. Catherine Zeta-Jones received threats from Dawnette Knight. She sent notes saying she was going to slice Zeta-Jones like meat on a bone and feed her to the dogs. Knight was charged in 2004 with felony stalking and 24 felony counts of making criminal threats.

Kathleen Thurston, a crazed fan wielding an electric razor, screamed "I love you" repeatedly as she chased the actor Hugh Jackman. Eerily, Jackman recognized Thurston as the woman he spotted outside his home and daughter's school. Chidi Benjamin Uzomah, Jr. was arrested at E! Studios for trying to enter Ryan Seacrest's car and carrying a switchblade. Uzomah, Jr. was sentenced to two years in state prison and ordered to stay away from the American Idol host for ten years. Robert D. Hoskins was sentenced in 1996 to ten years in prison for threatening to slit Madonna's throat from ear to ear if she didn't agree to marry him.

Moving from stalking to kidnapping and other nefarious dangers, Kelly Frank, a house painter at David Letterman's Montana ranch, was sentenced to 10 years for plotting to kidnap Letterman's toddler son as well as the boy's nanny. Victoria Beckham was the target of two kidnapping plots and one credible death threat. She was moved to a safe house by Scotland Yard after a plot to kidnap her and her child was discovered. Jonathan Norman, a paranoid schizophrenic fan, was found trespassing on Steven Spielberg's property. Police found photos of Spielberg and his family, curtain rods, duct tape, handcuffs, and a utility knife in Norman's possession. Norman expressed his ultimate intention to rape the director. While dining at a Lake Tahoe restaurant, Frank Sinatra Jr. was kidnapped, blindfolded, placed in a trunk, and driven to Los Angeles. After the Senior Sinatra paid the $240,000 ransom, Jr. was released unharmed. The perpetrators were eventually caught and the money returned.

If you feel you need security, don't skimp and don't wait. Most of the time, celebrities are treated well and admired for their contribution to the arts and our culture. But there are truly crazy people out there willing and ready to harm you. If there's even a chance that you are in danger (and almost certainly if you are high-profile and going to a public space), the cost of security is well worth the expense.

Mentor

I don't think I responded very well to the sudden
celebrity, the sudden fame, and the loss of privacy.
– David Schwimmer

While your celebrity may have happened as a result of a single event, stepping into a high-profile life is an evolutionary experience. Transitions unmanaged lead to regrettable decisions. The stark impact of fame is coming face-to-face with its challenges. It can be off-putting when the adulation seems like a threat liable to turn into the scrutiny of a Schadenfreude-prone media story in an instant. At those times, the red carpet can become a tightrope walk. Every talk show invitation can pose a potential risk and every adoring fan a potential threat. *The demands, pressure, and unrealistic expectations can be overwhelming.* Life is a challenge when you find it hard to stay grounded and sane in the seemingly insane world around you.

You need someone who can guide you as a wise confidant and help you stay focused and safe. Sometimes, you just need a confidential shoulder to cry upon. You need that someone to bestow a balanced perspective, give you a pragmatic approach to overcome challenges, and prevent you from making the same mistakes again and again. If you are a high-profile individual of any kind, a professional, skilled Mentor is the answer to most of your questions, even the rhetorical ones.

If you're depressed or suffering from a mental illness, see a therapist. Your mentor can help you determine if you need medical help. There is a profound difference between a depressed person and one who is discontented. Depression is a state of general unhappiness or despondency with regard to self and life. To be discontented is to be dissatisfied with your circumstance. See a therapist for depression. A mentor can help you gain clarity, shift perspectives, renew energy and motivation, and help you discover solutions, resolve issues, and champion your future.

As with all your trusted advisors, make sure strict confidentiality agreements are in place. Do not choose a mentor who is looking to create his or her own celebrity on your back and at your expense. I've had more than one client tell me how safe and secure it feels to know, with certainty, that nothing from our conversations will be sold to the media or chatted about at industry cocktail parties.

You want a Mentor who isn't recognized by the public or part of your social circles. Mentors have no vested financial interest in the offers you accept, so there are no conflicts of interests or cross-purposed agendas. A Mentor isn't there to become your BFF. She has her own friends, as do you. Your Mentor holds you accountable to your biggest vision, so she has the courage to tell you what you need to know instead of what you want to hear, even if you don't like her very much for doing so. She knows how to stand firm for the fearful inner child within.

As a Mentor to high-profile clients, it's an honor and privilege to work with talented, driven people like you who are on a mission to be the best they can be each and every day. I believe the greatest gift of the human spirit is the fullest expression of an individual's talents. Anything that diminishes that expression diminishes the quality and health of the society within which we live. I encourage my clients to stay mindful of their brilliance and the impact it has on the world. A thriving client is a joy to experience.

Chapter Six
The Bare Bones Cost of Fame

My problem lies in reconciling my gross habits with my net income.

– Errol Flynn

One thing about being famous is the people around you, you pay all their bills so they very rarely disagree with you because they want you to pick up the check.
– Charles Barkley

Celebrity is Expensive

Let's first take a look at what are your general personal expenses. There is a price to looking and feeling good. As you age, it becomes more costly. If you stay in the media, relevant over many decades, you may shell out three quarters of a million dollars or more just on skin care and surgical nip and tucks. This doesn't include hair, clothing, and make-up. Part of Jennifer Aniston's look is her fabulous hair. Coiffed by stylist Chris McMillan, who owns Chris McMillan The Salon in Beverly Hills, CA, rates for a simple haircut are around $600. Flying him in on location to do her hair for a movie premier, and all it entails, ran a bill for Anniston of around $50,000 after travel, hotel, styling costs of $2,000 per day, and a per diem. Celebrity makeup artist's fees start at $1,000 per day. It can add up, especially if you have a very active appearance schedule. While you get a lot of fabulous clothes and accessories for free, you still shop, luxuriously, to mirror the style of your brand image—and because, like most people, you like nice things.

Add in another few thousand dollars in monthly fees for personal training and private chefs. If you have children, you may be spending anywhere from $70-$130,000 for a top-notch, secret keeping nanny. For security and to keep prying eyes out, you can spend around a half a million dollars for on-duty armed security guards and a state-of-the-art camera system.

Now let's look at the bare-bones basic costs to run the business of celebrity. Much of your expenses will go to your team. Even if you're not a superstar, you still have basic business operating expenses. Depending upon your needs and level of activity:

Publicist: $4,000 to $15,000 per month

Lawyer: $600-$700 per hour

Agent: 10% of each deal they make on your behalf

Manager: 10% of earnings or more depending upon the level of service

It's easy to see how your expenses can quickly eat up your net profits. Get the most out of your investment by hiring well and running your business like a for-profit business that plans efficiently for your future. Generating a healthy profit will give you the expanded capacity to transfer some of your net-worth to non-profit causes that touch your heart.

Your Relationship With Money

I'm starting to feel like I have to cure my addiction to Hollywood money, because while it's delightful, it's also insidious.

– Alec Baldwin

Your relationship with money informs how you experience life and your deepest feelings about yourself and others. Take stock of your alliance with money. As Henry David Thoreau once said, "Wealth is the ability to experience life." If we think money is what will give us that ability, that's just not true. Think about the people you know, perhaps a friend, who feels anything but free. Perhaps she's living a life that's not her own. Thoreau knew, as we all must learn, that money is a useful expedient for certain things, but true wealth is the ability to enjoy and experience the extraordinary life you are living, every moment of every day, no matter where you are or what you are doing. If you are lucky enough to be a celebrity, money can grease the wheels and allow you to have experiences many people will never have, but it is your appreciation of your exceptional circumstances that will be your true wealth.

Observe your friends and associates with abundant financial means. Do any feel empty instead of full? Perhaps they lack meaning and purpose in life. Money can't guarantee how we will experience our abundant circumstance. Experiences are created from within, informed by your inner dialog that has its own perspective and relationship with reality.

To get to the root of your money relationship, we first have to define what money is. Money is just pieces of paper we've assigned a flexible value to. Today, it's more likely to be digits in a computer that get transferred from one computer to another. We invented money to improve our barter system. It was a lot easier to go to the marketplace with paper and coins in your pocket than to lugs beans, goats, cows, and chickens to trade for goods and services unavailable on your farm. Money also allowed people like you to get paid in something that wasn't beans or goats, and so society can now put a (high) value on artistic achievement.

When you put money under a microscope, you'll see that it's made up of atoms and molecules just like the comfy chair your sitting in. Just like your Loubouton stilettos or Patek Philippe watch. Your body is made up of atoms and molecules. Money at its essence is energy. And it is the energy you have around money that shapes your fears, anxieties, desires, needs, and insecurities about it.

We all learned some lessons about money as children, but they vary widely and aren't all necessarily good lessons. They also probably don't apply to your newfound level of wealth. You likely still hold these beliefs about money whether you're aware of them or not. Society is penetrated with beliefs about money. Perhaps you've heard *money is the root of all that is evil?* Well, if you think deep down inside that money is the root of all evil, then you're going to work very hard against yourself in maintaining wealth because you don't want to become or be seen as an evil person. Same thing with *rich people are greedy.* You'll feel a nagging sense of being conflicted because you don't want to be a greedy person. *Money doesn't grow on trees…its very hard to come by…there's never enough…*more is better and when more isn't better the solution must be even more! The mere fact that you believe something to be true doesn't make it true, at least not absolutely true without exception. Yet the beliefs we took on for ourselves serve as the foundation of what becomes your money personality. We all have a money personality.

There are many different money types. Some are healthy; many are toxic. They can result in bankruptcy, illness due to stress, and self-inflicted financial victimization. Given the primary focus of this book, I won't go into depth about the nuances of all the money types. I do want to address four very common unhealthy money types so you understand their attributes and can recognize whether or not you harbor some of them within you. I'm also going to describe a very healthy money type for the same reason and so you can model those attributes if you don't express them already.

First, there's the Spender. She overspends, brilliantly running up multiple credit cards. She shops 'til she drops so she can feel better about herself and how she perceives her circumstance. Typically, her immense closet is full of clothes, jewelry, and accessories, many of which still have the tags hanging from them. She believes that if she just buys this one more Hermes bag, then she'll be seen as good enough, respected enough, valued enough. And she wastes a lot of money in the relentless pursuit of *enoughness*. The irony is, shopaholics pile up belongings because they don't feel they belong.

Now, let me be clear. The ability to enjoy an abundance expensive luxuries is one of the reasons we're born creators. There is nothing inherently unhealthy or wrong with any purchase, no matter how extravagant. It's not *what* you buy, it's about *why* you buy it. If you buy because you like the beauty, utility, and you can easily afford whatever catches your eye—enjoy it! If, however, you're buying because you think it will somehow make you or the quality of your experience better, then you're really no different than the addict constantly searching for her next feel-good hit. Develop a self-worth that rivals your net worth and notoriety.

If you're not sure your buying motives ask yourself this: *If no one were to see me with it, beside it, in it, wearing it—or know that I have it—would I still buy it?* Assuming you're not investing in an ensemble to wear at an industry event, if your answer is *no*, rethink your purchase. What are you really trying to buy with that purchase? If your answer to that question is yes, chances are you're buying it to pleasure your healthy spirit, not your wanting ego.

Nothing outside of you can give you what you want and need the most. If you want to be seen as good enough, you have to feel and believe that you are good enough. If you want to be respected and valued, you have to first respect and value yourself. There isn't a couture bag in the world that comes packaged with self-respect.

Let's take a look at the Avoider. Bank statements and financial statements arrive never opened or read. Examining them may necessitate some decisive action, and that's terrifying for some people who aren't well versed in money management. What if a mistake is made? Avoiders aren't stupid people. They are often highly intelligent. They just avoid the topic of money, so they're not well versed in money matters. And they're too embarrassed to ask questions. So they either don't manage their money at all or they blindly had it over to 3rd party people to oversee: their spouse, an agent, or a financial manager. And we've all heard the stories where some of these Avoiders get the rude awakening one day only to find they're financial resources have been squandered by these third parties or—unwittingly—by themselves.

If the Avoider type is you, it's time to get responsible about your money. Ask questions and keep asking questions until you get answers you can understand. Seek expert advice and help. But play an informed role in strategy and decision making with regard to your financial future. Be the steward of your money instead of its (potential) victim.

Perhaps you're a Worrier. She worries. For her, money equals security and she just can't ever feel secure enough. She's terrified that her worse fear will come to be: that she will end up living in a box by the side of the road, that she'll become a bag lady. Her fear is way out of proportion to her financial status and abilities. She's frozen and can't make financial decisions, even if the obvious choice is in her best interest. She doesn't trust her own instincts, let alone those of a financial expert. She tends to hoard her money rather than leveraging it, sometimes creating her own self-fulfilling prophecy. She loses a lot of sleep worrying about money, to the detriment of her health and wellbeing.

If the Worrier is familiar to you, get a grip on your financial reality. Examine your fears. What's really going on? What is it you don't understand? Is your fear rational? If your fear is real, then it's time to take positive action and make sound decisions. Perhaps it's time to cut down on your spending. If your fear is irrational, then reach for a better perspective, one that will support you as you leverage your money to enrich your financial future.

When you look in the mirror do you see a Money Monk? For the Monk, money is the root of all that is evil or rich people are jerks. Monks repel money because they don't want to be evil or a jerk. Money is perceived as seductive in all the wrong ways. Monks don't value their product or service enough to create and sustain profits. Like the Avoider, the Monk shuns all tasks and discussions with regard to money, ultimately creating the self-fulfilling prophecy of poverty.

If you're a Money Monk, you'll be best served when you realize that money, like everything else, is the exchange you get for the value you've provided. Money by itself is neither good nor bad. What we have or how we use it may be judged positively or negatively. The more money you have, the more money you have to exchange for what you value most. If you want to help poor people, then you need to provide goods or services to people who have the money to pay you so you can exchange some of your profits for the time to work with the poor (or pay for goods and services that they need).

Finally, there's the Money Master. He creates his life from his heart motivated by intuition, inspiration, and passion. He values himself and appreciates the life he has. He spends his day masterfully creating what will enrich and empower the greater good of all, including himself. Money management is enthusiastically embraced because it serves as the means of exchange to do just that. He values himself and his talent, and he appreciates all that life has given him. What he appreciates, appreciates. With that attitude money naturally flows into his life as he continues to create abundance at home and in the lives of those he loves.

That was a very brief overview of some of the different money types. Be curious and dig deeper into what serves as the foundation of your money type. Keep the beliefs that are in your best interests; transform those that undermine your opportunity. You earned your money, and it's ultimately up to you to see that it's managed in your best interests. Invest in and spend your money in alignment with your values. Take a look at your checkbook and credit card statements. Do they reflect your highest priorities? If so, you're getting a great return on that investment. If not, it's never too late to make meaningful adjustments to your money habits.

Mind Your Money Matters

I always loved working as an actress, but I didn't understand why I couldn't just opt out of being famous. And then I realized you can, and I think I did. And eventually, I came to understand that you can do that and also keep working.

– Debra Winger

As a money earner you need to become a money minder. Otherwise, you may join the rags-to-riches-to-rags rollercoaster ride shared by many who've kept their eyes on everything but their finances. Overspending and financial mismanagement have crippled many high-profile individuals who've either ignored their advisors or allowed them to run amok with their wealth. It's your money, your future. You have the ultimate responsibility for its proper stewardship.

Just because you have an extraordinary talent doesn't mean you're automatically a savvy investor. Excessive spending and/or expensive legal troubles can also derail a direct path to a healthy cash flow and a strong portfolio. You don't have to look far to find a celebrity who is struggling with money woes.

In 2009, actor Nicolas Cage had an issue with the IRS for reportedly failing to pay $6.2 million in taxes. He sued his business manager for negligence and fraud, who countersued saying he warned Cage about his outrageous spending. An extravagant spender, Cage purchased a Gulfstream jet, castles in Germany and England, and a dinosaur skull, though his tax debt may well be unrelated to his spending. Piano-man Billy Joel has filed for bankruptcy three different times and lost about $90 million. He relied on his ex brother-in-law to manage his funds. Critical to minding your money matters is minding your money manager.

Game of Thrones star Lena Headey told TMZ in April 2013 that she had less than five bucks in her bank account after her nasty divorce and custody fight with her husband, Peter Loughran. She also took a $450,000 hit on the Hollywood Hills home she sold the year before. A bad restaurant investment and an ugly divorce from Loni Anderson forced troubled actor Burt Reynolds to file Chapter 11 bankruptcy in 1996. Fifteen years later, his mansion was foreclosed upon due to continued misguided investment decisions. Oscar winning actress Kim Basinger lost an $8 million lawsuit to Main Line Pictures for backing out of her commitment to the movie *Boxing Helena*. Not long after, Basinger had to sell Braselton, GA, the town she bought for $20 million. Rap icon MC Hammer earned over $33 million by 1991. By 1996, however, he was sitting on about $14 million in debt and declared bankruptcy. His excessive spending included a custom-built $30 million mansion, a Kentucky Derby racehorse, 17 cars, and a Boeing 727. His bankruptcy filing forced him to sell his extravagant home at a significant loss.

Cautionary tales like these occur far too often. Those in the high arch of an earning swing typically don't think financial devastation can happen to them. It can and does. Revenue highs will inevitably cool down. If you're monthly overhead outpaces your earnings, you can get into troubled financially waters very quickly.

Be realistic about your long-term earning potential. Recognize a windfall year for what it is: an earning boost not an average. Keep your business and personal expenses in line with a fairly conservative financial plan. Hire the most reputable advisors and keep a lid on their billings. Pay attention and learn. When in doubt, question. Look out for money sinkholes. Track and adjust your spending according to your fiscal fluctuations. Pay your taxes, and pay them on time to avoid stiff penalties and unnecessary legal expenses. Be smart. Put money away for that inevitable rainy day.

A Lesson From Pro-Athletes

*To many people spend money they haven't earned
to buy things they don't want to impress people they
don't like.*

– Will Smith

The constant need for admiration, acknowledgement, and validation can lead an individual down the road to bankruptcy. The ESPN documentary *30 for 30: Broke*, explored the detrimental effects of excessive spending by many sports celebrities. Many lavishly exhausted their financial resources in a lightly veiled competition to "be more by having more" than other pro-athletes. By the time they have been retired for two years, 78% of NFL players are bankrupt or broke. Within five years of retirement, 60% of NBA players are broke or are under financial stress.

What happens to these players that they can go from extreme wealth to bankruptcy? Players ascend from humble means and sign huge contracts on their first day. They become instant millionaires. Sadly, they are ill prepared to manage their assets. Other entities profit off of the celebrity, such as the university where they played college football, but there are currently no classes that provide players with assistance to navigate through the *experience* of instant wealth. The financial planning community chomps at the bit to manage a player's financial assets while ignoring or dismissing any growth in wealth of spirit.

Typically, young star athletes don't seriously consider that there will be an end to their wealth or fully grasp that their life as a player will end in a few short years. "What's next?" does not enter their minds as they become consumed with a lifestyle that also consumes them.

Often, the sports celebrity wants to "keep up" with other players, even if their contract doesn't compare. They will purchase the house/car/boat/jewelry that will earn the jealousy or respect they desire. They also enjoy extravagant nightlife and are known to frequent strip clubs. At the clubs, some players enjoy literally throwing money into the air, and they might spend $5,000-$10,000 in one night. They are chasing life high after high, and everyone else seems to be doing the same thing.

Michael Jordan's father is quoted in the documentary as having said, "Michael doesn't have a gambling problem. He has a competitive problem." This quote highlights the challenge of a celebrity who is struggling with a desperate need to fill an emotional void in an environment that makes gratification the central concern.

Some make the savvy move to get expert financial advice. Listening to that advice is not always part of the package. I've spoken with several financial consultants with a high-profile clientele, including athletes, who will inform the athlete that the restaurant, nightclub, or any other particular investment isn't a good idea, only to learn that the client is now the proud owner of soon-to-be defunct enterprise, loosing his investment or more in the process.

When the money and career ends, the celebrity experience also ends. It is not uncommon for a player's marriage to end, leaving the athlete with hefty monthly alimony and child support payments. Some former NFL players now have humble jobs in sales to merely stay afloat. It isn't uncommon to find hocked Super Bowl rings on E-bay. Unfortunately, the players need the funds the ring can procure for them. Adjustment to waning fame can be extraordinarily difficult, though it is often inevitable.

As for most people who've earned vast sums of money, the wealth didn't come with an education on how to manage it properly. It's one thing to hire professional help. It's another thing to comprehend and stay on top of the financial strategy they create for you. Your job is to make sure they understand your ultimate lifetime financial goals and what you value most, so they can align the strategy and financial tactics to achieve that outcome. It's your future, so give your full attention to your money matters.

Celebrity Begets Celebrity

The minute you start the process of deciding to make a film and you're communicating that vision to anyone, you're in the process of selling. If you don't understand that, you're not in show business. You're just not.

– Peter Guber

Network socially as a driven brand. The activity will get your farther faster than social networking, assuming you want a career of substance that sustains. Nothing is more expensive than a missed opportunity. Take advantage of your differentiation from *normal people*. As a celebrity, you're part of a members-only club. With an all-access backstage pass to those who can elevate and influence your career, you have incredible access. Optimize and leverage it. Celebrity begets more celebrity. Being an active participant and a genuine force among the coveted inner circle will raise your esteem within it.

Schmoozing expertly with the elite is much more than shaking hands and sharing cocktails and gossip. You can have a lot of fun that way, but you won't get much done to pump up your career. Rather, connect with purpose. Prepare. Go to each event with a plan. If you know in advance who will be there—people that you want to meet— reach that goal before you reach for your second glass of champagne. The bubbly can be your reward. If you're not sure who will be in attendance, assign yourself a number of new contacts to add to your web of relationships. Aim for three to five new people at a single event. It's a realistic and manageable goal, especially if you have a determined conversation with each new person.

The pursuit will also get you out of your comfort zone of spending the opportunity chatting with old friends and associates. Instead of talking about the subject of *me-me-me*, be refreshing by having a few targeted engaging questions about the person your meeting prepared ahead of time. The more you get them to talk about themselves, the more they'll remember you. Plus you'll discover interests you may have in common, which will come in handy later when you stay in touch.

Dress appropriately. Studies show that more than fifty percent of a good impression is based on how you look. Your hair, make-up, and radiant smile will be dazzling, no doubt. Entice the people you meet with your exquisite sense of style. Look the part that reflects your purpose aligned with type of affair you're attending.

Even in casual settings, be professional. If you want to connect, you have to look people in the eye—and they have to be able to look into yours. If this is an event where sunglasses rule, be bold and take yours off at the start of your networking conversations. You may find that your gesture will illicit the same in the person you're talking to—and a business relationship (at least) is born.

If you're Barbra Streisand, you can be assured the people you don't know will know you. There are a few others who can claim the same ubiquitous notoriety. If you're not in that group, introduce yourself with a handshake and offer your name and relevance (TV show or film you're in, political position, book authored, company founded, team and position played, etc.) Be clear, concise, and compelling in your summation. Even if the person you're meeting responds that they know who you are, the introduction shows your humbleness by not assuming everyone recognizes your face and knows your name.

Know why you want to meet a particular person. Have an agenda. Hollywood is especially known for its attitude of *what's in it for me?* Be ready to suggest how you may be a good fit for whatever endeavor they're working on. If there isn't a click, ask for an introduction to or referral to someone who might mutually benefit by a connection.

Lastly, follow up. Make a mental note or write it on your hand if you have to the key take away from the new interaction. Reach out on that point in a timely manner. As the months and years go by, find new reasons to touch base. Doing so will strengthen your connection and forge their sense of who you are and why you matter.

Be a Zen Master of Social Media

*All of it drives me crazy. I don't understand this need
to share. We almost exploit ourselves in order to feel
seen.*

– Scarlett Johansson

Even though your star has risen, you will always be a human
being. There will always be a part of you that wants to connect with
and belong to the pulse of the society in which you live. Social Media
provides an unprecedented opportunity for celebrities and the general
public to communicate directly. Never before has there been such a
level playing field of access with such a low barrier to entry.

When you've reached celebrity status, some everyday things
become delicate balancing acts, including your Twitter feed. People
start paying very close attention to your 140 character missives. Just
as its prudent to be more careful with how you act in public in the
real world, be careful with how you behave in the virtual world. The
Internet is a powerful communication tool, one that can connect you
with your fans in unprecedented ways. They can follow your every
online move with immediate access to each post as well as the backlog
of your submissions from days past.

You will eventually hit a wall of sorts when it comes to organically
gathering followers based on nothing more than your star power.
Only so many people will be naturally drawn to you and your brand.
You still have to give your followers a reason to stay engaged. Publish
worthwhile and entertaining content. Instead of just broadcasting
news about you, join the conversation—with fans and with fellow
celebrities who are influential and share your principles. It's okay to
be controversial, as long as you are well versed on the subject at hand.

A virtual face off may deliver a short-term trending status only to sucker-punch your reputation in the end. When in doubt, take the high road.

Just as birds of a feather stick together, so do celebrities. Take advantage of your relationships with other personalities for mutual benefit. Collaborate on a creative work and then cross promote said work on both of your networks. Or give your co-star a shout-out for her exemplary performance. Retweet their success, but stay away from their drama unless it's a rational show of support. Remember, text-based communications are often misinterpreted because the tone and intention of the expression are absent and the reader often imposes his or her own tone to the Tweet.

Use the tools of new media to your advantage. Maintain an active social network that is honest and true to your real self. Hire professional help to manage it if you need it, but stay on top of things. Tweeting is not much different than talking. Don't say things you will be afraid or ashamed to say in front of your mother or your friends.

There are other entities to consider partnering with through social media. Charities are the perfect partners for anyone wishing to enrich their public image. Pick a worthy cause—one you truly believe in—and offer your support. The charity can use its networks to promote your affirmation, and you can use yours to raise money for the cause. This sort of activity shows your generosity, compassion, and involvement in your community.

The rise of social networking also created a phenomenon where an unknown can claim center stage in the virtual public conversation while remaining at home wearing pajamas. Some of these online notables, such as MySpace queen Tila Tequila, have leveraged the online popularity to secure roles on reality television shows. Other, such as Havard Rugland a.k.a. *Kickalicious*, went from being a nobody to a YouTube sensation to pro-athlete with a spot on the Detroit Lions team. Sixth grader Greyson Chance became a bona fide overnight success with an amazingly good cover of Lady Gaga's *Paparazzi*. The amateur YouTube video attracted the attention of the music industry as viewership soared passed the 15 million mark. Without the Internet, Justin Bieber, comedian Bo Durnham, songwriter Esmee Denters, and actor Liam Sullivan may still just be performing in their bedroom.

People from all over the world are tapped into social media. Admittedly, there is a little bit of the exhibitionist and the voyeur in all of us. Otherwise how would you explain the popularity of social networking websites? The public desire to announce to their friends where they are and what they are doing right now is matched only by the compulsion to know what others are doing, especially the famous.

In this medium, though, the masses have final cut on what they choose to reveal: namely, their highlight reel. You are likely to find your behind-the-scenes and editing-bay-floor cuttings showcased as a running commentary that defines and shapes your persona, whether you like it or not. In today's world, where everyone and anyone with a cell phone camera may have the chutzpah to just make it up and report it as so, celebrity brand managers have less and less control over the presentation and direction of their client's public image. The structure of the social networking sites underscores what separates ordinary people from celebrities. Everyone has friends. As a celebrity, you have followers.

What adds to a publicist or manager's challenge is sometimes clients don't heed the optimal rules of engagement in social networking. They tweet their rants, trysts, drunken epiphanies, and various viral blathering that require immediate damage control. There's a reason press agents are often called *suppress agents.*

You should take the necessary precautions, which include getting professional assistance to ensure that your public image is managed in an appropriate manner. This involves incorporating a system of checks in place to ensure that a momentary lapse of attention or a weak moment when anger or rage can overcome an otherwise pleasant public personality does not shatter the public image that you have worked hard to build. This means your every move in public will need to be carefully monitored or even rehearsed so that you do not slip up.

Does it seem very complicated? It is. You pay your publicist and manager, if you have one, a lot of currency for their expertise. For gosh sakes, get your money's worth. Follow their instructions when it comes to your direct communications with your fans and the media.

Celebrities spark today's most engaging online conversations. For you, the real gold in social media is a new channel for earning revenue through endorsements. High profile personalities have been used in marketing campaigns for a long time. What's new is celebrities can now directly drive customer acquisition, not just provide a brand halo. Companies such as Shoedazzle (Kim Kardashian), The Honest Company (Jessica Alba), and Beachmint (Kate Bosworth, the Olsen Twins and others) work directly with celebrities to expand brand influence and sell more products.

You can join Charlie Sheen and Snoop Dogg to be among those who are paid $2,500 to $8,000 per sponsored tweet. That's a lot of dough for just typing 140 characters. If you amass millions of followers, you become the upper echelon of the tweet elite. Ad.ly is the largest social media celebrity endorsement company. They connect the top brands in advertising with the biggest names in pop culture. The most expensive sponsored tweet as of this writing was a call by Charlie Sheen for a Tiger Blood intern who would apply through Internship.com. The $50,000 tweet generated nearly 100,000 clicks to the company's website and over 80,000 people applied for the position.

Social media has also become a valuable tool, and at the same time, the biggest nemesis of the political and corporate executive culture. Politicians and known industry leaders reach out to the Twitterverse to speak to and for their constituents, customers, and to boost their own name awareness. Social media strategies influence political campaigns by rallying the voting community and provide juicy content for the media to exploit. While slow to start, corporate CEO's are starting to use social media to better communicate with their customers and put a "face" to their brand.

Politicians and CEOs

Be a yardstick of quality. Some people aren't used to
an environment where excellence is expected.
— Steve Jobs

Celebrity can create perils for high-profile politicians and CEOs. Politicians and industry executives face similar challenges to managing their personal brands. First, you both face a massive audience. Second, you have huge personal financial and emotional stakes in the game. The risks of failure or of reputation damage are enormous.

Personal branding relies on creating and deploying your powerful message to the right market through the right channels. The result of a positive name association effort is having customers—or voters—willingly invest their time, money, and emotions in your product. The product, of course, is you, beyond your company or your political platform.

You can build or break an empire through your actions or inactions, your charisma, and your adherence to core values. Be concerned about your individual legacy while working to enrich the value of your name and improve its market position and reputation. Ensure that the values of your company or campaign reflect the tenets you dearly hold within your entity and externally to the public at large.

The key to personal success beyond your current position is getting people to be customers for life, rather than allowing them to switch brands every few years. Your job is to build your reputation for longevity and strength. You are the ambassador of your brand, so your actions speak as loudly as the quality of the product or service. If you work with a Board of Directors, stockholders, or voters, you may be replaceable within the company. The industry as a whole will recognize and welcome what your name and reputation can bring to the table. Be a role model, a mentor, and a trusted voice in the community.

Manage your trademark identity carefully. The twenty-four hour news cycle and the multitude of real-time news sources make it impossible for anyone to ignore the absolute requirement for honesty and accountability. Expect your worst hair day and your most horrific verbal gaffe to be tweeted around the world in minutes, if not seconds. As a politician or high-profile executive, become a watchful of and positive participant in of the public conversation about you.

Even though it is impossible today to completely control what is said or believed about you, those who direct the message and the media come out on top. Being in control of your own life has nothing to do with being controlling. It's more about having the fortitude to direct your scenarios and monitor your reactions.

With intention, show up consistently with clear and consistent principles to maintain the trust of your audience. Executives leading their companies into landmines, corporate political mazes, and downright criminal activity litter the headlines. Politicians placing personal ambitions above the desires of their constituencies experience record low popularity numbers.

Discern the difference between confidence and aggression. Confidence emanates from within where aggression is an external projection. Confidence is free from worry where aggression is birthed in fear and doubt. Hubris and inflated egos are cancers to your profession. Parallel to any other form of high-profile persona, you serve yourself best when you keep it real, stay grounded and sprinkle inspiration wherever you go.

The CEO Celebrity

A brand for a company is like a reputation for a person. You earn reputation by trying to do hard things well.

– Jeff Bezos

Celebrity status can be achieved with a senior level executive position through controversy or solid good business acumen. By making something of yourself, you can leave a profound mark in the world and in the company you lead. Big name executives, including Jeff Bezos, Richard Branson, Steve Jobs, Sam Walton, Mary Kay Ash, Mark Zuckerburg, Steve Ballmer, Michael Bloomberg, Michael Dell, Warren Buffet, Donald Trump, and Carly Fiona, have earned public figure status as a result of their roles in leading companies. Entry into this esteemed business group begins when journalists attribute and report a company's positive performance as a direct result of actions by the CEO. It can also occur when a high-ranking leader sullies his or her reputation amidst allegations of professional or personal impropriety.

As a star executive, you enjoy prestige and power, higher compensation, and personal benefits. You have an intangible mystique that can serve as an asset for your company. Your place within the company may lead to an increase in stock price, increased employee morale, and a positive shift in the company's image. You also present a risk because if you're reputation is damaged so is the public estimation of the company brand. The business becomes only as good as you are. Avoid the spotlight when prudent. Unless you have the charm, charisma, bravado, and persistence of Steve Jobs, whose charisma was rightly credited with introducing products with such a convincing fliar that his keynotes were streamed worldwide and his pitch so compelling it was labeled a "Reality Distortion Field," stick with company talking points that are relevant and meaningful to your customers and suppliers. Keep your statements believable and your promises within a realistic realm of possibility.

While you may be excited about your product or position, be mindful of how you express your enthusiasm. There is a fine line between being seen as someone expressing confident excitement and some crazed nut doing a "monkey dance," as Microsoft CEO Steve Balmer was called during the opening of his presentation at Microsoft's 25th Anniversary event in September 2000. The spectacle was captured on video, uploaded to YouTube, seen and re-seen by millions of people and is still being talked about today as a black mark on the slowly circling drain of the once almighty Microsoft corporation.

On the flip side, you don't want to be the person who can make the moon landing seem dull either. Start by giving people a reason to listen to what you have to say. How will your message benefit your audience? First and foremost, answer the unspoken question on your audience's mind: "Why should I care?" Strike an emotional chord that will motivate people to embrace or take positive action upon what you have to say. Tell stories to engage your audience and make a deeper connection. Keep it simple, and speak in plain English so you can easily be heard and understood. Paint a picture of what *could* be so that you have a greater chance of selling your dream.

As a politician or CEO, you can be viewed as an icon or a scoundrel. If your job performance or behavior is inconsistent, you will face personal media scrutiny. Those close to you may have to endure probes into their personal and public lives merely because of their association with you. Even well respected CEOs have been known to tarnish their reputations in one way or another. Bill Gates was portrayed as ruthless and without compassion, Jack Welch was exposed in the media for having an extramarital affair, and Martha Stewart is still fighting to recover from her time in the big house for her insider trading conviction.

What do you do when your good name takes a hit? Be honest. Apologize only if you can do so and mean it. If you do say you're sorry, do so with a clean, straightforward, and consistent communication. Apologize publicly to anyone and everyone who was negatively impacted by your actions. Make amends instead of excuses. There is no circumstance where it is wise to trade jabs with your critics.

The Celebrity as CEO

If you come up with a great idea and then put a great business plan with it, and you can get the capital, then the sky's the limit.

– Magic Johnson

There are a number of stars that have become CEOs. Perhaps you are, or will become, one of them. Many have leveraged their celebrity equity and business savvy to make millions. At the pinnacle is perhaps Oprah Winfrey. The queen of daytime talk was once valued at $2.4 billion. As a cultural icon, her brand has become a quintessential symbol of success. Among the many businesses, she created the *Oprah Winfrey Show*, *O Magazine*, and the Oprah Winfrey Network. Her production company, Harpo Productions, develops feature films and television and radio programming. Oprah has also launched the highly successful careers and, ultimately, businesses of Dr. Phil, Rachael Ray, and Dr. Oz. Her magic wand has catapulted unknown authors into bestsellers and turns her recommended products into an overnight household necessity.

Hall of Fame basketball player Magic Johnson is an ace on the court and in the business arena as well. Chairman of Magic Johnson Enterprises, he lists his holdings in Burger King franchises, Starbucks, movie theaters, TGI Friday's, fitness centers, travel agencies, and a real estate development firm. He's also inked a minority ownership interest in the Los Angeles Lakers. Johnson, through his business empire, is a man on a mission to serve as a catalyst for driving unparalleled business results by fostering community and economic empowerment, making available high-quality entertainment, products, and services that answer the demands of ethnically diverse urban communities.

Adding to her triple-threat talent as an actress, singer, and dancer Jennifer Lopez is also an astute businesswoman. In addition to commanding $15 million and more per movies, Lopez is making millions in producing movies, making music, and designing fashion. She was one of the first celebrities to launch her own clothing line. The business also sells perfume and jewelry. Lopez is also the Chief Creative Officer of NUVOtv, the first English-language network for today's modern Latinos. She went on to found the mobile phone company Viva Móvil that caters specifically to Latinos.

Shawn Corey Carter, aka Jay Z, is an American rapper, record producer, entrepreneur, and investor. At this writing he's received seventeen Grammy Awards for his musical work and is consistently ranked as one of the greatest rappers of all time. As a businessman, Jay-Z owns the 40/40 Club, is the creator of the Rocawear clothing line, and has a minority stake in the NBA's Brooklyn Nets. The former CEO of Def Jam Recordings is the co-founder of Roc-A-Fella Records and the founder of Roc Nation. In an interview he stated, "My brands are an extension of me. They're close to me. It's not like running GM, where there's no emotional attachment." According to another interview with journalist Anthony DeCurtis of *Men's Health*, staying true to yourself is a common theme in Jay Z's philosophy of success. He believes that what separates winners from losers is a commitment to a single proposition: You are the product. If people believe in you, they will believe what you create.

Big, bold, irreverent egos that operate for the greater good create ecosystems of opportunity. While generating millions of dollars for themselves, they create hundreds, if not thousands, of jobs. As a celebrity CEO, be yourself, follow your passion and be nice. If you can't be gracious, at least be civil. Yes, you're important. The business would be a small shadow of what it is without your importance. The people who work for you want to feel important, too. Give them that gift, and they will serve you well personally and financially.

Lead as you would like to be led. Put company interests ahead of your personal desires. If you are overly self-involved or out of alignment with company core values, your value to stakeholders dissolves. As a leader, seek the level of performance as CEO as you do as a talent. Infuse your company with a meaningful purpose and contribution to society. It's okay to earn a lot of income by giving back. The more you receive, the more you have to give.

Chapter Seven
Lift As You Climb

I'm a true believer in karma. You get what you give, whether it's bad or good.

— *Sandra Bullock*

If you haven't got any charity in your heart, you have the worst kind of heart trouble.

— *Bob Hope*

My story of success and failure isn't just about music and being famous. It's about living and loving and trying to find purpose in this crazy world.
                                                              – Wynona Judd

Paying It Forward

As a celebrity with means, you naturally seek to leave a lasting impression upon the world. While you play a vital role in your particular industry, you have the opportunity to play an essential part in our society. Fame is a gift that affords you the opportunity and the responsibility to give back by becoming more than just a headline name. Like it or not, you are a role model. You have enormous reach and power; use it to do good for generations to come.

You didn't make it to where you are without help from many others along the way. Somewhere along the line you got a break, a helping hand, or a lift up during your climb. Now, it's time to repay that gift by helping others and paying it forward. Lift as you continue to climb the ladder of personal and professional achievement. Leverage your platform to transform the lives of others.

The world isn't changed by people who sort of care; it's changed by people who passionately, audaciously care. You may have had an exceptional experience that moved you to become devoted to a cause. Or you may be motivated to support a cause simply for attention. Those who limit their contributions to checkbook photo-ops will soon become transparent to the public in their veiled attempts at publicity or a clever tax deduction. Trevor Neilson of the Global Philanthropy

Group will tell you that you have to earn your stripes in philanthropy if you are a celebrity, and it takes homework.

What matters to you? If you're not sure, understand that your purpose in life is not a thing, it's a natural unfolding. What matters to Matt Damon is every fifteen seconds a child dies because of a lack of clean water and sanitation. Moreover, there are 2.5 billion people on Earth who don't have clean water to drink. To get an upfront view of this kind of deprivation, Damon spent quite a bit of time in Africa, India, Ethiopia, and Haiti to see for himself how people live under such conditions. He met with the locals, shook their hands, and listened to their stories. As his children get older, Damon plans to bring his family with him on these trips so they can learn about how other people live and experience the gift in giving back through his Water.org foundation that focuses on water and sanitation.

Instead of a persona, become a philosophy in action. Do more than just speak about what you think is important. Walk your talk. Back up your words with action. Otherwise, you'll leave an incomplete legacy—a hollow shell of what you wish you had done. And you'll know the pain of what that awareness delivers. Despair is a cheap excuse for avoiding one's purpose in life, and a sense of purpose is the best way to avoid despair. Use your blessings. While many people feel called to make a difference, you are in the position to do this on a grander scale than most.

When you help others, you help yourself. The gift is in the giving, as they say. You'll know you've made a difference by leveraging your name and influence to serve the greater good. Leaving your mark on the world by investing your resources, time and energy will feed your spirit.

Get your hands in it. While financial commitments support an organization's goals, they do little to make you feel relevant from the inside out. Anyone with money can donate cash. It takes real dedication to make an impact that matters most in a passionate purpose.

Your celebrity can turn a cause into a household name. Rock and roll legend Jon Bon Jovi knew early on that he wanted to use is fame to do more philanthropically. He quickly realized that while simply writing a check helped others (and provided a tax deduction), it did nothing to make him feel like he was making a personal impact. Philanthropy requires reciprocity. Beyond your good intentions, you have to participate. You have to invest your time and energy beyond your financial resources. Bon Jovi established the Soul Foundation to combat issues that force families and individuals into economic despair. Its mission is to fight against hunger and homelessness. The foundation provides safe and affordable housing options so that the families and volunteers can make a difference, rebuild pride in one's self, and one's community, one person at a time.

When you grant critical resources, do so generously, without hesitation or expectation of a return. You were once on the receiving end of someone else's gifts. Remain humble enough to remember how even a small consideration opened a door, removed a roadblock, or revealed a more promising path.

If you haven't already, find a cause or a project and then take a stand. The currency of stardom is fame itself, so invest it well. Invest the whole of you. Everyone needs to feel fulfilled and useful, and you are no different in this regard. You are not our work, and while your work is a resume of what you've done, it does not define who you are as a person. Your character is determined by what you leave behind and what you've given to others—even through the kindness of your words.

You may need guidance and assistance to set up our philanthropic efforts and in lending your names and our energy to ideals you support. If you're not sure where to start, look into some of the consulting firms devoted to helping you manage your goodwill. Ben Affleck, Rachel Ray, Yao Ming, Barbra Streisand, Nicole Richie, Avril Lavigne, Ben Stiller, Demi Moore, and Ashton Kutcher are just a few celebrities who've paid experts to strategize their philanthropic endeavors.

If you decide to establish a foundation for giving, realize that running a foundation takes discipline and a unique set of skills. Empower your organization by hiring an experienced advisor to position it for maximum impact. These experts will help you develop a plan for giving that helps maximize tax benefits as well as handle the research and development to make sure the intent of the foundation is realized to make a real impact.

True leaders lead by changing the lives of others for the better. You create your legacy daily simply through your actions and your deeds. It is lazy and unwise to leave your legacy to chance. Create it mindfully and with foresight every day. Dare to connect with others, dare to be more than your brand, and dare to drive the dream as you create the reality of your vision.

Join the following people who are also making a significant difference by lifting as they climb. The list of those who positively leverage their fame and fortune to leave permanent footprints in the sands of time would fill a vast volume.

In 1981, Johnny Carson established the John W. Carson Foundation to support children, schools, and the environment. The foundation continues to give millions of dollars each year to issues Carson cared about most. Angelina Jolie and Brad Pitt created the Jolie-Pitt Foundation to support human rights issues. Jolie is a Goodwill Ambassador for the United Nations, focusing her attention on the plight of refugees around the world.

Joe "Joey Pants" Pantoliano and Tony Goldwin are co-presidents of *The Creative Coalition* to bring together artists and entertainers to tackle issues of direct importance to the arts and entertainment community, including First Amendment rights, public funding for the arts, and arts education in public schools.

George Clooney is on a mission to stop the human rights atrocities in the Darfur region of Sudan. Much of his support and personal participation is spent on helping those suffering from poverty. He visited the Nuba Mountains with the ENOUGH Project, launched by the Center for American Progress to end genocide and crimes against humanity, to document the barbaric acts of the Sudanese government on its own people.

Ashley Judd began working as an activist in college, and she was deeply affected by the conditions of women in Southeast Asia. She now travels extensively in support of campaigns to ease poverty, increase public health, human rights, and to address social justice and women's rights.

Aviva Drescher, along with Mary Amons, supports with their time, energy, financial resources, and generous heart her cousin Fran Drescher's organization Trash Cancer/Cancer Schmancer. Drescher is the National Spokesperson for the One Step Ahead Foundation, an organization that helps children with disabilities build self-esteem and self-confidence through athletics, the Challenged Athletes Foundation (CAF) that provides grants to athletes with a physical disability, Live4life whose mission is to help those affected by melanoma, and So Gay So What, a grassroots campaign that celebrates individuality as it spreads the message of love, acceptance, support, and respect in the LGBTQIA community.

Sting co-founded The Rainforest Foundation with his wife, Trudie Styler, to save rainforests in South America. An annual benefit concert is held for the Foundation. A Columbian tree frog, Dendropsophus Stingi, was named after him in recognition of his commitment and efforts to save the rain forest.

Hugh Jackman participated in a humanitarian mission to Ethiopia with the group World Vision. This trip included a meeting with a local coffee farmer, which changed the way he looks at the world. As a result, Jackman launched Laughing Man Worldwide, a food and beverage company. The company donates 100% of its profits to charity. Jackman promotes causes that strengthen third-world communities and supports local farmers.

John Legend is passionate about providing quality education to children around the globe as a means to break the cycle of poverty. He started the Show Me Campaign, and began a Poverty Action Tour with Dr. Jeffery Sachs. They tour universities to encourage social, personal, economic, and educational growth. The two asked communities and students to commit to helping charities fight poverty.

Bono, the iconic lead singer for U2, is well known for his activism on causes such as Third World poverty and the African AIDS crisis. When it comes to fighting poverty and hunger, he is constantly in direct contact with world leaders and policy makers in his quest to make the world a better place. He was on Forbes magazine's Generous Celebrity List for his work with Debt AIDS Trade Africa (DATA) and helped to create the ONE Campaign to rally Americans, one by one, to fight the emergency of global AIDS and extreme poverty.

Sandra Bullock regularly donates large sums of money and lends her name and support to Doctors Without Borders. Ben Affleck has worked with Hilary Clinton to address childhood mortality rates. He founded the Eastern Congo Initiative, to work with women and children of the Democratic Republic of Congo. Childhood mortality rates there are appalling, with 15% of the nation's children dying before the age of five. Beyoncé and her family started a mission to help people affected by disasters. She stated, "Reaching out and touching lives is incredibly empowering. That's why I want my fans to experience the joy of making a difference by helping someone else." Don Cheadle, George Clooney, Brad Pitt, Matt Damon, David Pressman, and Jerry Weintraub collaborated to create Not on Our Watch. The organization focuses global attention and resources towards ending mass atrocities around the world. They have worked on these issues surrounding Darfur and the Sudan, among others.

To learn more about how those with fame and fortune are making a profound difference, I invite you to visit www.LookToTheStars.org, a site launched in 2006 by Steve and Myrlia Purcell to publicize the many wonderful things celebrities are doing to help the world. They hope to help charities by inspiring other stars and fans to follow the esteemed example of others in their community.

In addition to giving to charities, you can mentor someone who is traveling a similar journey. Give them the benefit of the lessons you've learned along the way. Giving back by sensing an obligation to your community or industry is a good and decent thing. *Contributors* rather than *consumers* are the cornerstone of a thriving civilization.

Mentors are important because they champion a higher vision of the potential in each individual they serve. Mentors set an example of what's possible and can hold others accountable to achieving what may be believed impossible.

You can mentor a single person or do as pop singer and actor Usher has done. He founded Usher's New Look, a nonprofit established to help create avenues for young people to enter the business side of the sports and entertainment industries. Basketball legend Magic Johnson, along with hip-hop artist Common, BET (Black Entertainment) Chairman and CEO Debra Lee, and Coca-Cola spearheaded a nationwide apprenticeship campaign to motivate and develop careers of young people.

Steven Spielberg, who counts Jerry Lewis as a mentor, said Lewis taught him the importance of mentoring. Dancer and singer Donald O'Connor mentored actress Bonnie Franklin. Quentin Tarantino, director, calls crime fiction writer Elmore Leonard a real mentor. Renowned acting coach Stella Adler was a mentor to Marlon Brando. Gary Cooper mentored Kirk Douglas. Jack Lemmon, Jason Robards, Robert Carrelli (Chatsworth High dram teacher), and John Graham Spacey (uncle) were mentors to Kevin Spacey. Comedian Frank Shuster mentored Lorne Michael, executive producer of *Saturday Night Live*. Gary David Goldberg was a pivotal mentor to Michael J. Fox. Bob Fosse influenced Melanie Griffith. I could go on. Most well-known, accomplished, successful people can identify people in their lives who empowered their career through mentorship. Be among those who make a difference with your inspiring example and sage advice. You'll get much more out of it than you give. Those you serve will get resources. You'll get the satisfaction and fulfillment that comes with living a useful and purposeful life.

It's not that I'm not grateful for all this attention. It's just that fame and fortune ought to add up to more than fame and fortune.
– *Author Robert Fulghum*

Don't be afraid to give up the good for the great.
– *Kenny Rogers*

Afterword

*People assume I'm out there having this great life,
but money doesn't erase the pain. When you're young
you barrel through life, making choices without
thinking of repercussions. A few years down the line,
you wake up in a certain place and wonder how the
hell you got there.*

– Jennifer Lopez

The purpose of this book is to help you ride the dragon of fame and stay grounded, admired, and inspired as you thrive in a high-profile life and career. Creative people frequently don't think of their craft as a business to build and a mindset to sustain. My hope is that with this book, I've been able to remove uncertainty, fear, and frustration and empower you to enjoy and express the highest version of your brand persona and authentic self.

The lifelong journey of managing fame and dealing with celebrity takes time, fortitude, and commitment. You live and work inside walls that you create. I'm challenging you to climb the wall. To do that, you need to develop a solid foundation to stand upon and establish a very good set of principles and parameters. Working collaboratively helps to shape and stabilize ideas, creativity, and the masterful stewardship of your good fortune. Doing this will insure its sustainability and growth.

Fame is a rollercoaster ride where insecurity, fear, and doubt will derail you each and every time. Just because people see your face all over the place doesn't mean they see you. Perhaps you've lost sight of yourself somewhere along the way. It happens to the best of us, especially in the pressure cooker business of celebrity. Or you may want to develop or rekindle your internal flame. I know you want to make the most out of your claim to fame or you wouldn't bother to get out of bed in the morning—let alone read this book.

Your time here on this Earth is priceless. Be the author, director, producer, and star of your life story. To do that, you have to take ultimate responsibility for it all. The word author is from Old French *auctor*, *acteor*, "originator, creator, instigator" or from Latin *auctorem* "enlarger, founder, master, leader," literally, "one who causes to grow". As the author of all that is you, you have the power and right to determine to direct and command your destiny.

There's great power that comes with being the creator of all you experience and achieve. You will never be a victim to anyone or anything. From the things that don't work out so well, you'll learn what to do differently for better results the next time. From the things that come together exquisitely, you'll discover the recipe to bake that cake again and again.

In addition to your divinely given power, you have star power. It's not what you have that counts, its how you use it. Empower your fame, fortune, and future. Use your influence as the prophetic wizard Merlin used his wand to shape-shift the celebrity and life experience you want instead of what you tolerate or face today.

Your best business asset is your accountability partner. Working with someone who can help you stay focused, on purpose, and on track to create your career and life by design rather than default will keep you grounded, admired, and inspired every step of the way. You've already proven great things are possible. While you live and breathe, you're not done yet. Expand the Universe of what you believe is possible for you—and get out of your own way.

If you can consistently hold yourself accountable to your greatness without finding excuses and reasons for well intended yet misguided choices, that's fantastic. In fact, if you can do this for yourself, you're already doing it. If you're like most people, no matter how skilled an intelligent you are, having someone shine more light on your circumstance and steadily hold up a mirror to your highest potential can power you through challenges. It can make all the difference in the world.

This is your time of times. The choices you make today create your tomorrows. Any book can give you information and advice. It's up to you to apply what is relevant to you and your goals in your daily life. No one else can do this for you. Yes, it's a lot of work and there's no law that says work has to be unpleasant or arduous. When done purposefully, labor becomes pleasure as you play full out in the zone, firing masterfully on all cylinders.

You know deep within you are destined for something grand. It calls to you as it dares you to step boldly out of your comfort zones. It's scary, yet what you fear the most is often what your heart is begging you to become. Answer the call. Rise above challenges, circumvent roadblocks, and keep on keepin' on with a firm hand on the helm of your destiny.

Where you go from here is entirely your choice. You can toss this book aside, wing-it, and see what happens, or you can invest in building a solid foundation for your success, from the inside out. My contribution is to put you in control of your life and destiny and give you the tools and training to grow and expand in what you love doing.

Only a few sustain the championship of their highest potential. Be someone who does. You already have everything you need to stay grounded, admired, and inspired in the crazy world of fame and fortune. You'll find it within: your innate wisdom, talents, and the fortitude and power of your conviction.

As John Lennon sang in his song *Instant Karma*, "Who do you think you are, a superstar? Well, right you are." Shine on and on and on and on.

Author's Note

I hope you enjoyed reading this book, and that it serves as a resource you come back to whenever you're looking for help, support, or insight. I invite you to visit me online at **www.FameMentor.com** for additional information and inspiration or get in touch with me to help you ride the dragon of fame, navigate demands, immobilize pressures, and maximize your opportunities, as you stay grounded, admired, and inspired throughout your extraordinary life.

I don't go to premieres. I don't go to parties. I don't covet the Oscar. I don't want any of that. I don't go out. I just have dinner at home every night with my kids. Being famous, that's a whole other career. And I haven't got any energy for it.

– Gary Oldman

Acknowledgements

This is a book that I craved to write, felt compelled to share, and am eager to celebrate. It wouldn't have been possible without the enduring and unwavering encouragement of my clients, whose names shall remain confidential. You know who you are. The insights and experiences they've shared for this book are gifts to those who boldly follow in their footsteps.

My deepest thanks go to Dale Launer, meritorious comedy screenwriter and all-around grounded good guy. Your astute behind-the-scenes insights and perspective offered me a private and personal glimpse into the attitudes, fears, and deepest desires of those who roll the dice in this game of fame. We're due for another round at Caffe Luxxe soon.

To Aaron Drucker for his endless patience, dedication to excellence, and creative wizardry as editor, book interior, and cover designer extraordinaire. Any words of appreciation I express would be an inadequate tribute to your contribution.

To Ben Watkins, prolific writer, actor, producer, and director. I couldn't have asked for a more brilliant living example of someone who rides the dragon each and every day, holding himself responsible for and accountable to his *Why*. His candid perspective helped shaped the narrative in ways I could not have accomplished on my own. My appreciation for your generosity of spirit is everlasting.

I'd like to express my deepest appreciation for the heart-centered amazing women and Reality TV stars Mary Amons, Aviva Drescher, Kari Wells, and Lana Fuchs for their powerful example of how it's possible to remain rooted in your promise and vision, leveraging their exposure to do more good in the world. These amazing women stayed true to the conviction of their soul even when the odds were stacked against them—on and off camera. It's an honor and a privilege to know you.

To Penny Douglas Furr, a dear friend and family law attorney, who shared her high-profile divorce case experiences and perspective with me at length, even into late night hours, as I researched this book.

To my serendipitous friend and ace Personal and Executive Assistant Deon Lowery, your above and beyond standard of service is unprecedented. Your mission to help and teach those who follow in your footsteps is admirable and necessary. I do believe the next lunch is on me.

To the veteran and esteemed Agent Susan A. Simons, thank you for giving it to me straight about what sells and what doesn't in the world of Reality TV programming. Your directness is only rivaled by your passion and commitment to your client's career and continued success.

To Murray Garrett, eminent Hollywood photographer, author of photographic books *Hollywood Moments* and *Candid: A Photographer Remembers* and a true mensch. It was an honor to visit with you as you shared your unprecedented all access passport experiences with me. Each time I gaze upon one of your stunning quintessential Hollywood photographs, I forget to breathe. Hopefully I have risen to the occasion of your wisdom to add a little fanfare and excitement to the launch of this book. Give my warmest regards to your lovely wife, Phyllis, who has traveled the journey with you for over sixty years. I look forward to our next visit.

To Richard Taite, Founder and CEO of Cliffside Malibu and co-author of *Ending Addiction for Good*. It has been an honor and privilege to get to know you and the extraordinary level of service and passionate care you provide each and every person who enters your treatment facility and therapeutic programs.

. To Arun Raj and Ed Robertson who helped me organize, shape, and edit the manuscript through its many iterations. I know I drove you crazy at times as I tried to get organized. Thanks for hanging in there.

To my patchwork family, Adriel, Julia and Hakim Terbeche, Addison Williams, Taylor and David Sampson, Aubyn Williams, Libby Calejo, Marjorie Kuhn, Bliss Krekel, Keyomars and Monica Fard, Wendy Posner and Bo Berg, and John and Bernadette Capellaro. I love you more than I'm able to adequately express. Your inspiration rekindled the flame of my mission, enabling me to move steadily forward when I felt overwhelmed in analysis paralysis.

Finally to my husband and most treasured friend, Al Satterwhite. How and why you tolerate my zealous spirit is beyond me. Your love and loyalty is immutable. In my feverish frenzy to research, write, and complete this book there were many days when I neglected to thank you. Can I make it up to you with bottle of Turley? Now, go feed the cats, please.

The best fame is a writer's fame. It's enough to get a table at a good restaurant, but not enough to get you interrupted when you eat.

- Fran Lebowitz

Select Bibliography

The quotations and high-profile examples throughout the book come from a variety of research on- and offline. Much of the material was sourced through personal confidential interviews with clients and industry experts. The 2009 Journal of Phenomenological Psychology scholarly article (Issue 40 pp. 178-210) *Being a Celebrity: A Phenomenology of Fame* by Donna Rockwell, Michigan School of Professional Psychology, and David C. Giles, University of Winchester was a part of this body of research. Where confidentiality isn't breeched, a specific interview source is cited. The Kevin Mazur documentary, *$ellebrity*, was viewed, as it provided documented support of client experience claims as they were revealed to me. The video gave me pause and an awareness of my role in supporting widespread celebrity privacy invasions as a paying consumer of celebrity oriented material.

Braudy, Leo, *The Frenzy of Renown: Fame and Its History*, New York, NY: Vintage Books, 1986, 1997

Butt, Ty, *Gods Like Us*, Toronto, Canada: Pantheon Books, Random House, 2012

Currid-Halkett, Elizabeth, *Starstruck: The Business of Celebrity*, New York, NY: Faber and Faber, Inc., 2010

Halpern, Jake, *Fame Junkies: The Hidden Truths Behind America's Favorite Addiction*, New York, NY: Houghton Mifflin Company, 2007

Marshall, David P., *Celebrity and Power: Fame In Contemporary Culture*, Minneapolis, MN: Regents of the University of Minnesota, 1997

Redmond, Sean and Su Holmes, *Stardom and Celebrity: A Reader*, London, England: SAGE Publications, 2007

Being famous is having the power to really implement positive change in the world, and it gives you the power to do what you want. I'm really grateful for it because I can play music and people will listen.

- Sean Lennon

About The Author

Valery Satterwhite grew up in the magic city of Miami Beach, Florida. Her father, Dr. Michael Meyer Gilbert, was a world-renowned forensic neuro-psychiatrist—a playboy with a reputation for narcissism who self-destructed amidst a highly publicized scandal. Valery learned firsthand the paradox that can come from life lived in the bright lights of fame and fortune. Bright lights tend to cast long shadows.

As an adult, she continued to recognize the unique emotional and practical challenges that come with a life thrust upon the public spotlight. Valery was determined to help those powerfully stay grounded, admired, inspired, and sane in a seemingly insane world. Through years of training, study, and endless hours of research and client consultations, Valery offers the sum of that wisdom in this powerful guide. She hopes readers will use it to light up the world with the power of their celebrity.

Valery holds a Master Level Certifications in Neuro-Linguistic Psychology (CM.NLP), is a Certified CORE Multidimensional Awareness Facilitator (Emotional and Social Intelligence), and a Certified Sports Psychology Coach. She lives in Los Angeles, CA with her husband, photographer Al Satterwhite, and two Zen masters—both of them cats.

For more about Valery and her work to help those who want to ride the dragon of fame masterfully so that they can stay grounded, admired, inspired, and sane in a seemingly insane world, please visit www.FameMentor.com.

www.ingramcontent.com/pod-product-compliance
Lightning Source LLC
La Vergne TN
LVHW051456080426
835509LV00017B/1780